FIELD

GW00983095

MICROSOFT
WORKS 3
FOR WINDOWS

PUBLISHED BY

Microsoft Press
A Division of Microsoft Corporation
One Microsoft Way
Redmond, Washington 98052-6399

Copyright © 1994 by Siechert & Wood, Inc.

Library of Congress Cataloging-in-Publication Data
Field guide to Microsoft Works 3 for Windows /
    Siechert & Wood, Inc.
        p.   cm.
    Includes index.
    ISBN 1-55615-620-0

    1. Integrated software. 2. Microsoft Works for Windows.
I. Siechert & Wood, Inc.
QA76.76.I57F54   1994
005.369--dc20   94-14766
                                                    CIP

Printed and bound in the United States of America.

1 2 3 4 5 6 7 8 9 QBP 9 8 7 6 5 4

Distributed to the book trade in Canada by Macmillan of
Canada, a division of Canada Publishing Corporation.

A CIP catalogue record for this book is available from the
British Library.

Microsoft Press books are available through
booksellers and distributors worldwide. For further
information about international editions, contact your local
Microsoft Corporation office. Or contact Microsoft Press
International directly at fax (206) 936-7329.

Acquisitions Editor: Lucinda Rowley

Project Editor: Tara Powers-Hausmann

Technical Contact: Mary DeJong

Writers: Stan DeGulis, Carl Siechert

FIELD GUIDE TO

MICROSOFT
WORKS 3
FOR WINDOWS

Siechert & Wood, Inc.

The Field Guide to Microsoft Works version 3 for Windows is divided into four sections. These sections are designed to help you find the information you need quickly.

1 ENVIRONMENT

Terms and ideas you'll want to know to get the most out of Works. All the basic parts of Works 3 are shown and explained. The emphasis here is on quick answers, but most topics are cross-referenced so you can find out more if you want to.

Diagrams of key window components, with quick definitions, cross referenced to more complete information.

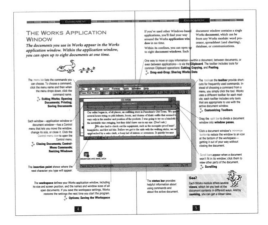

Tipmeister

Watch for me as you use this Field Guide. I'll point out helpful hints and let you know what to watch for.

15 WORKS A TO Z

An alphabetic list of commands, tasks, terms, and procedures.

Definitions of key concepts and terms, and examples showing you why you should know them.

Cross references to related topics.

Quick identification of icons and Works modules.

Step-by-step guides to performing most Works tasks.

167 TROUBLESHOOTING

A guide to common problems—how to avoid them, and what to do when they occur.

177 QUICK REFERENCE

A full list of tools that you can use to customize your toolbar for fast access to Works features.

189 INDEX

Complete reference to all elements of the Field Guide.

INTRODUCTION

In the field and on expedition, you need practical solutions. Fast. This field guide provides just these sorts of lightning quick answers. But take two minutes and read the introduction. It explains how this unusual little book works.

WHAT IS A
FIELD GUIDE?

A Field Guide—to North American Forests, to Equatorial Africa, or to Microsoft Works—is a pocket-sized handbook that provides quick, short, and easy-to-use answers for those pesky questions that come up when you're trying to get about your work.

This Field Guide to Microsoft Works is different from all the other computer books on the shelf. Its illustrations work like road maps that point you exactly to the information you need. If you're a new user, the Field Guide gives you step-by-step instructions that will have you using Works like a pro in no time. If you're an experienced user, the Field Guide provides you with a concise quick reference to all the Works terms, tasks, and techniques.

WHEN YOU HAVE
A QUESTION

When you have a question about how to do something with Works, turn to the Field Guide's Environment section. The Environment works like an illustrated index. For example, if you want to know how to work with a database, flip to pages 10 and 11, and you'll see an illustration of a Works database. The captions for the different parts of the picture describe all the things you can do with databases and point you to the exact entries in the Works A to Z section that describe each task in detail.

WHEN YOU WANT TO KNOW MORE

The second part of the Field Guide, Works A to Z, is like an illustrated dictionary to Microsoft Works. It contains more than 200 entries in alphabetical order that describe terms and give you the steps to perform tasks. (Often, you'll be able turn directly to Works A to Z to find the information you need.) For example, to learn how to have Works dial the phone for you, read the **Dialing Phone Numbers** entry.

WHEN YOU HAVE A PROBLEM

The third section of the Field Guide, Troubleshooting, is where to turn when something doesn't work the way it seems like it should. This section of the Field Guide describes the most common problems that new or casual Works users come across, and gives you one or more solutions to fix each problem.

HINTS FOR USING THIS FIELD GUIDE

This Field Guide uses several conventions to help you find your way around:

- When you see a task or term in **boldface**, it means you can find information about that task or term in the Works A to Z section.

- When you see the ⁂ symbol followed by a term or task, it means that term or task in the Works A to Z section contains some additional information related to the topic at hand.

- Throughout this Field Guide, you'll see these four icons: 🐾 🖥 🗄 🖳 . They are the same icons you see on the Works Startup screen. They tell you which of Works' four modules and document types—Word Processing, Spreadsheet, Database, or Communications—a term or task applies to.

- In some places in this Field Guide, you'll see tools like this: 📋 . The tool buttons show you a shortcut way to perform a task: click its button on the toolbar. (To change the tool buttons that appear on your toolbar, check out **Customizing Toolbars** in the Works A to Z section of this Field Guide.)

ENVIRONMENT

Need to get the lay of the land quickly? Then the Environment is the place to start. It defines the key terms you'll need to know and the core ideas you should understand as you begin exploring Microsoft Works.

THE STARTUP DIALOG BOX

The Startup dialog box first appears when you start Microsoft Works. You'll summon it often because it provides a signpost that points the way to many Works features and to the documents you create with Works.

Select the New & Recent Documents button when you want to create a new **document** or open an existing document.
New Documents

Select the Open An Existing Document button when you want to open an existing document that's not shown in the Recently Used Files list.
Exporting Documents; Filenames; Opening Documents

Select the Use A Template button when you want to create a new document based on a stored **template**, a "skeleton" document that can save you time and promote consistency among your documents.
AutoStart Templates; Letterheads

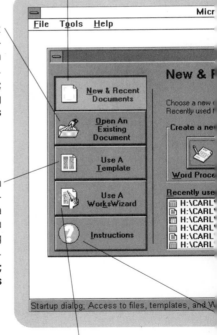

Select the Use A WorksWizard button when you want to use a **WorksWizard**. WorksWizards guide you through the process of creating a specialized document, such as a letterhead, or performing a task, such as a **mail merge**.

Actually, the very first time you start Works, you'll see a welcome screen that gives you an opportunity to take a guided tour of Works. Press T to take the tour if you like. But if you're adventuresome—and you wouldn't have bought this book if you weren't, right? —press S to skip the welcome screen and not be bothered with it again.

Your Works session then begins with the **Startup dialog box.** The Startup **dialog box** goes away after you use it, but you can bring it back by clicking the Startup Dialog tool on the **toolbar.**

Starting Works

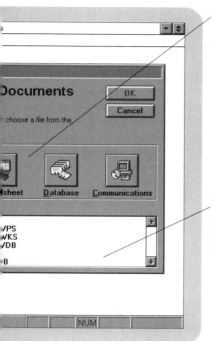

To create a new document, choose the button for the document type you want to create.

Works maintains a list of the last eight documents you've used. To reuse one of them, double-click its name in the list.

The Instructions button just tells you how to use the Startup dialog box—the same information that appears on this page. If you need more information about using Works, use the online **help**.

Cue Cards

THE WORKS APPLICATION WINDOW

The documents you use in Works appear in the Works application window. Within the application window, you can open up to eight documents at one time.

The menu bar lists the commands you can choose. To choose a command, click the menu name and then when the menu drops down, click the command name.

❖ **Exiting Works; Opening Documents; Printing; Saving Documents**

Each window—application window or document window—has a Control menu that lets you move the window, change its size, or close it. Click the Control-menu icon to open the Control menu.

❖ **Closing Documents; Control-Menu Commands; Resizing Windows**

The **insertion point** shows where the next character you type will appear.

Micr

| File | Edit | View | Insert | Format | Tools |

Times New Roman 12

CD.WD

SAFAI

Our safari began in, of all places, an outl several hours trying on pith helmets, boo vary only in the number and position of the inevitable vine swinging, but they did We also had to check out the e knapsacks, and first aid kits. Before we approached by a sales clerk, a bony lad

Page 1

MOUNTAIN.WKS IMAIL.WCM

Press ALT to choose commands.

The **workspace** defines your Works application window, including its size and screen position, and the names and window sizes of all open documents. If you save the workspace settings, Works restores the settings the next time you start the program.

❖ **Options; Saving the Workspace**

If you've used other Windows-based applications, you'll find your way around the Works **application window** in no time.

Within its confines, you can open up to eight **document windows**. Each document window contains a single Works **document**, which can be from any Works module: word processor, spreadsheet (and charting), database, or communications.

One way to move or copy information—within a document, between documents, or even between applications—is via the **Clipboard**. The toolbar includes tools for common Clipboard operations: **Cutting, Copying,** and **Pasting**.

Drag-and-Drop; Sharing Works Data

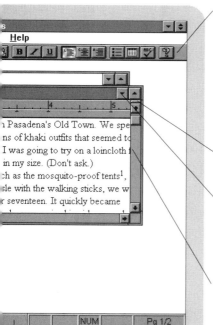

The tools on the **toolbar** provide shortcuts for frequently used commands. Instead of choosing a command from a menu, you simply click the tool. Works uses a different toolbar for each module; each toolbar includes only tools that are appropriate to use with the active document window.

Customizing Toolbars

Drag the split bar to divide a document window into **window panes.**

Click a document window's minimize button to reduce the window to an icon at the bottom of the workspace—getting it out of your way without closing the document.

Scroll bars appear when a document won't fit in its window; click them to view other parts of the document.

Scrolling

The **status bar** provides helpful information about using commands and about the active document.

See?

Each Works module offers several **views**, which let you look at the document contents in different ways. And by **zooming**, you can get a closer view.

5

WORD PROCESSOR DOCUMENTS

The Works word processor module not only lets you process words, but you can add charts, tables, pictures, and other elements to embellish those words.

The **ruler** lets you see and modify the indent and tab-stop settings for the current paragraph.

🐾 **Indents and Alignment; Margins; Page Setup; Tabs**

Your pages can include **headers and footers**, which you can use to print **page numbers**. You might also want to include the date and **time**.

🐾 **Special Characters**

Probably the most important thing in a word processor document is the words.

🐾 **Copying Text; Deleting Text; Drag-and-Drop; Editing Text; Entering Text; Moving Text; Replacing Text; Selecting Text; Undo**

You can insert **charts** or other objects anywhere in your document.

🐾 **Adding Pictures; Embedding and Linking Existing Objects; Embedding New Objects; Object Linking and Embedding**

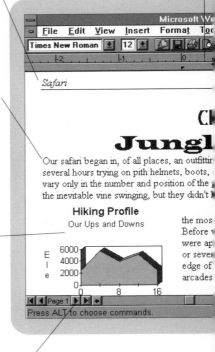

View different parts of a document by clicking the page buttons or the scroll bars.

🐾 **Bookmarks; Finding Text; Go To; Scrolling**

At its core, the word processor module is a very capable processor of words and text. It offers extensive text **formatting** options, a built-in **spelling checker**, automatic **bulleted lists**, multiple **text columns**, and powerful search-and-replace capabilities. But the word processor module is also the best place to see how Works integrates information from different modules: You can embed a chart or table from the spreadsheet module, a picture from the **ClipArt Gallery** or Microsoft **Draw,** or even a pop-up reminder from **Note-It.**

You can use a variety of **fonts** in your Works documents.

Changing Fonts; Points; WordArt

Paragraph-formatting options let you control the appearance of **paragraphs** and ensure that certain paragraphs stay on the same page.

Whether you write for a professional journal or just letters home to Mom, you can use features such as **footnotes** and **endnotes**.

Works can smooth out ragged edges by hyphenating words.
Ending Lines; Hyphenation; Nonbreaking Spaces; Word Wrap

Your friends and colleagues don't have Works? Not to worry. You can import and export documents for **Microsoft Word, WordPerfect,** and **Write.**
Exporting Documents

What about business documents?

Works has you covered, whether you want to print **letterheads, envelopes,** or **mailing labels.** And you can use **mail merge** to incorporate information from a Works database.

SPREADSHEET DOCUMENTS

The spreadsheet module simulates an accountant's ruled ledger sheets, but you don't need a green eyeshade to quickly and easily perform complex calculations on numbers.

The **formula bar** shows the **formula** or **value** in the active cell.
- **Calculating Formulas**

A cell is identified by its **column** letter and **row** number.
- **Cell Address; Names; Range**

The **active cell** has a heavy border (the **cell selector**), and its address appears to the left of the formula bar.
- **Selecting Cells; Selecting Columns and Rows**

Numbers or formulas you enter always go in the active cell.
- **Editing Cells; Entering Numbers; Filling Cells; Fill Series**

Formatting numbers lets you display numeric information in a convenient and familiar form, including **fractions, percentages**, and **scientific notation**.
- **Alignment; Currency Symbols; Date Formats; Time Formats**

| | Micr |
| File | Edit | View | Insert | Format | Tools |

Arial · 10

B10 =B8/B9

HISTPRI2.WKS

	A	B	C
1		Price per $	
2		1994	19
3	First	60 1/2	42
4	Second	51	44
5	Third	53 5/8	48
6	Fourth	59 1/4	57
7			
8	Net earnings	$171,420	$27,6
9	Shares outstanding	60,399	60,4
10	Earnings per share	$2.84	$0.
11	Price/earnings	21	1
12			

Press ALT to choose commands, or F2 to edit.

You can change the overall appearance of a spreadsheet in many ways. You can adjust the **column width, row height**, and **margins**. Or add **headers and footers**, including **page numbers**.
- **AutoFormatting; Gridlines**

8

The spreadsheet module is a whiz at performing mathematical calculations. And it can present the numbers in the form of colorful **charts**, which can enhance understanding of the numbers even among left-brained people.

The spreadsheet is a grid of rectangles called **cells**. The cells are where you put numeric **values** or **formulas** that perform calculations.

Formulas can also include **functions**, which let you perform complex calculations.
.: **Arguments; AutoSum**

Help

HISTPRI2.WKS - 3-yr comparison

Fabrikam, Inc.
Price per Share

First   Second   Third   Fourth
Quarter-end closing price

1994   1993   1992

NUM

You can change the appearance of information in spreadsheets and charts by **changing fonts**.
.: **Bold Characters; Italic Characters; Points; Underline Characters**

You can highlight cells by adding **borders**, **patterns**, and **shading**.

Works can create **charts** based on spreadsheet information.
.: **Chart Formatting; Chart Types; Editing Charts**

Chart text that accompanies a chart can include titles, axis labels, and legends.

You can embed Works spreadsheets and charts in word processor documents and database **forms**.
.: **Exporting Documents; Lotus 1-2-3; Microsoft Excel; Sharing Works Data**

You can change the arrangement of a spreadsheet's rows and columns.
.: **Deleting Columns and Rows; Inserting Columns and Rows; Sorting Rows**

DATABASE DOCUMENTS

The Works database can keep track of information—lists of customers or friends, store inventory, baseball card collections, and so on.

The information about each item in your database constitutes a **record**. In **list view**, each record occupies one row; in **form view**, only a single record is visible.

❖ **Adding Records; Deleting Records; Editing Records; Go To**

Each record is divided into **fields**, each holding a single piece of information.

❖ **Adding Fields; Deleting Fields; Hiding Fields**

In form view, the active field is indicated by reversing its colors; in list view, the active field is highlighted with a heavy border.

❖ **Selecting Cells; Selecting Columns and Rows**

Dress up your **forms** by **adding pictures, charts**, or objects from **WordArt, ClipArt Gallery, Draw**, or **Note-It**.

❖ **Embedding and Linking Existing Objects; Embedding New Objects; Object Linking and Embedding**

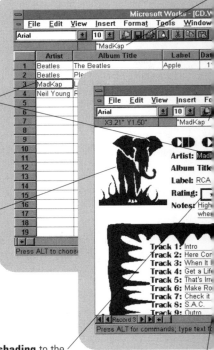

You can add **borders**, **patterns**, and **shading** to the background of fields, labels, or the entire form.

To the right of each **field name**, a **field line** shows you where to enter data.

❖ **Entering Data; Filling Cells; Fill Series**

You view and modify the information in the database module, but you can also merge database information into a word processor document—handy for **envelopes, mailing labels,** and other **mail merge** projects. The database module offers two basic views

of your data: **form view,** which emulates a paper input form, and **list view,** which displays data in a spreadsheet-like tabular format. Its two other views (**report view** and **query view**) allow you to sort and select records based on criteria you specify.

The **formula bar** shows the **value** or **formula** in the active field. Formulas can also include **functions**, which let you perform complex calculations.

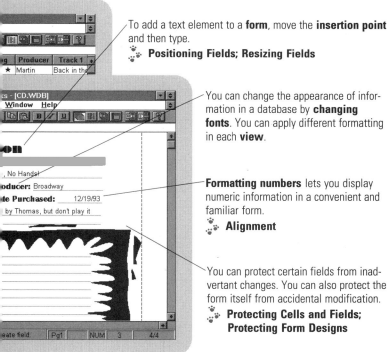

To add a text element to a **form**, move the **insertion point** and then type.

❖ **Positioning Fields; Resizing Fields**

You can change the appearance of information in a database by **changing fonts**. You can apply different formatting in each **view**.

Formatting numbers lets you display numeric information in a convenient and familiar form.

❖ **Alignment**

You can protect certain fields from inadvertant changes. You can also protect the form itself from accidental modification.

❖ **Protecting Cells and Fields; Protecting Form Designs**

A **report** produces printed output that includes only the fields you want, sorts and groups records, and can include calculations such as the number of records in each group, the total value of a certain field, and so on.

❖ **Report View; Sorting Records**

A **query** lets you find certain records and hides records that don't match your criteria. Hidden records are not included in database views, reports, or mail merge operations.

❖ **Finding Records; Hiding Records; Query View**

COMMUNICATIONS DOCUMENTS

The Works communications module lets you use a modem and a telephone line to connect to online services, electronic bulletin boards, and other computers running a similar communications program.

Before you begin a communications session, you must establish various settings that match your modem's capabilities and the settings used by the computer you want to connect to.

Communication Settings; Modem Setup; Phone Settings; Protocol; Terminal Settings

```
                    Microsoft Wo
  File   Edit   View   Settings   Phone

Connection initiated. . . Opened.

Welcome to MCI Mail!

Dow Jones introduces simplified
pricing!  New pricing begins on
April 1, 1994.

For details type HELP DOW JONES PR

Today's Headlines at 4 pm EDT

--3M, Union Carbide To Contribute
     $463 Million To Implant Fund
--Stocks Firm; Dow Gains 14 Points
     Looking Toward Inflation Data

Type //BUSINESS on Dow Jones for d

MCI Mail Version V13.0.B

     There are no messages waiting
     You have  1 active AUTOFORWARD

Command: _
```

Press ALT to choose commands.

The document window shows text that you send and receive during a communications session.

Capturing Text; Sending and Receiving Text

You can also send any file that you have saved on disk to the other computer, or receive a file from the other computer. When you do so, a message box appears that monitors the progress of the file transfer; the actual file contents never appear on your screen.

Sending and Receiving Files

A communications document isn't made up of information that you type in a document window. Instead, a communications "document" stores all the information necessary to make a connection to a particular online service, along with any **scripts** you create. (The information that you send or receive during a communications session is discarded at the end of the session unless you save it to a file.) The commands to enter the connection information are all on the Settings menu.

To connect to another computer, choose the Phone Dial command, click the **Easy Connect** toolbar button, or choose the Tools Sign-on command.

·:· Dialing Phone Numbers

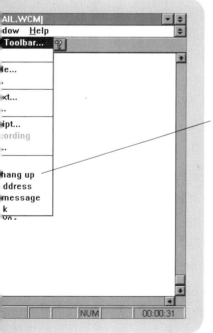

You can automate repetitive communications tasks by recording your actions as a **script**. After you record (and edit, if necessary) a script, you play it back by choosing its name from the Tools menu.

13

WORKS
A TO Z

Maybe it's not a jungle out there. But you'll still want to keep a survival kit close at hand. Works A to Z, which starts on the next page, is just such a survival kit. It lists in alphabetic order the tools, terms, and techniques you'll need to know.

A

Absolute Cell References

An absolute cell reference describes a specific location in a spreadsheet. An absolute reference always refers to the same **cell** regardless of where in the spreadsheet you move or copy the cell that contains the reference. To create an absolute reference, use a dollar sign before the column letter and row number, like this: A1.

Mixed Cell References; Relative Cell References

Active Cell

The active cell is the spreadsheet **cell** or database **field** that you are currently working with. It is the cell in which the text, numbers, or **formulas** you type are entered. The active cell has a highlighted border around it, and its address appears in the left portion of the **formula bar**.

Adding Columns and Rows

Inserting Columns and Rows

Adding Fields

You can add a **field** to a database in either **form view** or **list view**.

This view's for you

Using form view to add a field is usually easier and has several advantages over using list view:

- In form view, you insert the field and name it in one swell foop. In list view, you must first insert the field and then choose the Edit Field Name command to name it.

- You can specify the field width and height when you add a field in form view. In list view, you must first insert the field and then choose the Format Field Width and Format Record Height commands to adjust the size.

- When you add a field in form view, the added field appears on the form where you clicked. If you add the field in list view and then switch to form view, the added field appears at the very top of the form (superimposed over any field that's already there) waiting for you to drag it into position.

Adding a Field in Form View

To add a field in form view, follow these steps:

1 Click where you want the new field.

2 Choose the Insert Field command.

3 Type a name for the new field and adjust the field width and height as you want them.

4 Choose OK.

Your form reappears with the new field highlighted. To adjust the new field's position, simply drag it where you want it.

Adding a Field in List View

To add a field in list view, follow these steps:

1 Click the **field name** at the top of the column to the right of where you want to add the new field.

2 Choose the Insert Record/Field command to insert a blank field.

3 Choose the Edit Field Name command.

4 When the Field Name dialog box appears, type a name for the new field.

5 Choose OK.

Adding Pictures

To add a picture from the **ClipArt Gallery** to your word processing document or database **form**, follow these steps:

1 Position the **insertion point** where you want the picture.

2 Choose the Insert ClipArt command.

3 When the ClipArt Gallery dialog box opens, select the picture you want and choose OK. (Or simply double-click the picture.)

Draw; Moving Objects and Pictures; Resizing Objects and Pictures

Adding Records

You can add a **record** to a database in either **form view** or **list view**.

Adding a Record in Form View

To add a record in form view, follow these steps:

1 Scroll to the record before which you want to add a new record.

2 Choose the Insert Record command.

Works presents a new blank record and renumbers all succeeding records.

Adding a Record in List View

To add a record in list view, follow these steps:

1 Click the record number to the left of the row below where you want to add the new record.

2 Choose the Insert Record/Field command to insert a blank record.

A

Address Book WorksWizard 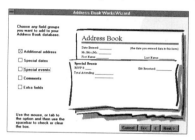 The Address Book
WorksWizard helps you create a database of names, ad-
dresses, phone numbers, and other information that you
can use to print **envelopes**, **mailing labels**, or form letters—or just look up addresses and phone numbers when
you need them. To use this WorksWizard, follow these
steps:

1 Choose the File WorksWizards command.

2 When the Startup dialog box appears, select Address Book.

3 The WorksWizard presents a series of options so you can set up
your database just as you want it. When you've made your selection in each dialog box, choose Next > to continue.

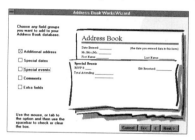

4 When you choose the last option, the WorksWizard offers to create
your database. If you're satisfied with the choices you made,
choose Create. The WorksWizard creates your address book as you
designed it and presents the first record for you to begin entering
names and addresses.

If you want to reconsider some of your choices, choose the < but-
ton to back up to the previous screen, or choose the |<< button to
start over again.

 Mail Merge

Alignment Alignment refers to the way Microsoft Works positions the labels and values in a spreadsheet or database. Unless you tell it otherwise, Works aligns labels and text entries to the left, and number and date entries to the right.

To change the alignment of any item, follow these steps:

1 Select the items whose alignment you want to change.

2 Choose the Format Alignment command.

3 When the Alignment dialog box appears, select the alignment options you want:

Option	What it does
General	Aligns text to the left and numbers and dates to the right
Left	Aligns the selection to the left
Right	Aligns the selection to the right
Center	Centers the selection
Slide to Left	(**Form view** only) Slides the selection to the left on the form, eliminating blank space, when you print
Wrap Text	(Not available in form view) Wraps the selection to the **field** or **cell** width, changing the height of its row as needed
Top	(Not available in form view) Aligns the selection with the top of its row
Center	(Not available in form view) Aligns the selection with the center of its row
Bottom	(Not available in form view) Aligns the selection with the bottom of its row

 Different views = different alignment

The alignment you select for a field applies only to that view, allowing you to specify a different alignment in list view, form view, and report view.

✦ **Column Width; Formatting; Indents and Alignment; Resizing Fields; Row Height**

A

Annotations

Note-It

ANSI Characters
ANSI (short for American National Standards Institute) characters include all the characters on your keyboard plus many special characters such as paragraph marks, bullets, mathematical symbols, and accented characters. These nonkeyboard characters are sometimes called extended characters.

Each ANSI character is assigned a code number, which you use to enter the character. To see a list of the ANSI characters and their codes, refer to the Extended Characters appendix in the Microsoft Works *User's Guide.*

Inserting ANSI Characters

To insert an ANSI character that is not on your keyboard, hold down Alt and type the character's code number using the numeric keypad. (You must type the code's initial zero, and you must use the numeric keypad; the number keys above the letter keys will not work.)

Need a map?

If you're the visual type (and who isn't?), you can use the Windows Character Map application to paste special characters into your documents. To do so, switch to Program Manager and open the Accessories group. Double-click the Character Map icon to open Character Map. Then select the character you want and choose Copy to place the character on the Windows **Clipboard**. Return to Works, and paste the Clipboard contents into your document.

Application Window
An application window is a window that holds an entire application, such as Microsoft Works. An application window can contain several **document windows**.

Switching Windows

Arguments

An argument is the information that a **function** needs to perform its task. An argument can be a **value**, **cell address**, **range** of cells, or even another function. When you insert a function, placeholders for the required arguments are shown in parentheses following the function name in the **formula bar**. For example, the SUM() function needs to know what cells to sum up. Its arguments, therefore, are cell ranges, shown in the formula bar like this: SUM(RangeRef0,RangeRef1,...). Replace each placeholder with an appropriate value or reference.

ASCII Text Files

ASCII (short for American Standard Code for Information Interchange, doo dah, doo dah) text files are files that contain only text characters, no hidden formatting codes.

ASCII files are "bare-bones," "lowest-common-denominator" files, useful for transferring information between programs or over the phone lines when the receiving program or computer cannot accept a formatted file. The information may not look pretty after you transfer it, but it usually beats retyping it when that's your only alternative.

Binary Files; Exporting Documents; Opening Documents; Saving Documents

AutoFormatting  AutoFormatting allows you to quickly apply presentation-quality formatting to a selected portion of a spreadsheet, or to a whole spreadsheet. To format with AutoFormat, follow these steps:

1 Select the group of **cells** you want to format.

2 Choose the Format AutoFormat command.

3 Select the format you want. As you select each format, the Sample box shows you an example.

4 When you've decided on a format, choose OK. Works applies the format to the selected cells.

AutoStart Templates Want to create a professional-looking document quickly without any hassle? AutoStart templates are the answer. Works AutoStart templates contain predefined formats for a wide variety of documents. To make selecting the template you want easy, Works divides AutoStart templates into three groups: Business, Personal, and Education. Works further divides each group into several categories.

To use an AutoStart template, choose Use A Template from the **Startup dialog box**, or choose the File Templates command. Then select the group, category, and template you want and choose OK.

❖ **Templates**

AutoSum

The AutoSum tool allows you to quickly total a **row** or **column** of numbers in a spreadsheet. To use the AutoSum tool, follow these steps:

1 Select an empty **cell** at the end of a row or column that contains the numbers you want to total.

2 Click the AutoSum tool. Works searches first up and then left for cells to include in the **formula**, and then proposes the cell **range** to be summed in the **formula bar**.

3 If the proposed range is correct, click the AutoSum tool again to enter the formula in the selected cell. If the range is not correct, edit the range shown in the formula bar, and then click the AutoSum tool to enter the formula in the selected cell.

Binary Files

Binary files are files that contain graphics, formatting codes, or any unusual characters. Microsoft Works documents, most word processor files, and program files themselves are all examples of binary files.

> ∴ **ASCII Text Files; Sending and Receiving Files**

Bold Characters

To change characters to **bold**, select the text (or the cells that contain the text) and then press Ctrl+B or click the Bold tool.

Bookmarks

Bookmarks allow you to quickly jump to a particular place in a document. Like a real bookmark, you can insert a Works bookmark at any place in a document you like. Then you can quickly return to that place at a later time, simply by jumping to the bookmark.

Inserting a Bookmark

To insert a bookmark, follow these steps:

1 Move the **insertion point** to where you want the bookmark.

2 Choose the Insert Bookmark Name command.

3 When the Bookmark Name dialog box appears, type a name for the bookmark.

4 Choose OK. Works inserts a hidden bookmark with the name you typed at the insertion point.

Jumping to a Bookmark

To jump to a bookmark, follow these steps:

1 Choose the Edit Go To command, or simply press F5.

2 When the Go To dialog box appears, type or select the name of the bookmark you want.

3 Click OK.

 Go To

Borders

 You can add borders around paragraphs in a word processor document, around fields or labels in a database **form**, or around **cells** and cell **ranges** in a spreadsheet.

Adding a Border

To add a border, follow these steps:

1 Select the item or items around which you want a border.

2 Choose the Format Border command.

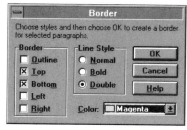

3 When the Border dialog box appears, choose the border type, color, and line style you want.

continues

25

Borders *(continued)*

Removing a Border

To remove a border, follow these steps:

1 Select the item or items from which you want to remove the border.

2 Open the Format menu and choose Border.

3 When the Border dialog box appears, do one of the following:

- For a word processing document, clear the check box for each border you want to remove.

- For a database or spreadsheet document, choose the empty line style (the topmost line style box).

Borders in database forms

When you add borders in a database **form**, Works adds a border around each individual label or **field** that you select. If you want a single border to surround several labels and fields, choose the Insert Rectangle command. You can then use Format Border to format the border around the rectangle. To move or resize the rectangle, see **Moving Objects and Pictures** or **Resizing Objects and Pictures**.

 Shading

Bulleted Lists

You can create a bulleted list quickly by using the **toolbar**, or you can use the Format Paragraph command to add a bullet to paragraphs with custom indents.

Creating a Bulleted List with the Toolbar

1 Select the paragraphs you want to include in the list.

2 Click the Bulleted List tool.

For each paragraph, Works adds a bullet at the beginning of the paragraph and indents all the text one-quarter inch from the left **margin**.

C

Creating a Custom Bulleted List

1 Select the paragraphs you want to include in the list.

2 Choose the Format Paragraph command.

3 Select the Indents And Alignment tab.

4 Mark the Bulleted check box, set the indents as you want them, and then choose OK.

Works adds a bullet and an invisible tab character at the beginning of each paragraph, with left and right indents as you set them.

Removing Bullets from a Paragraph

The bullet that Works inserts is a special Works character that you cannot select or delete in the usual way. To remove a bullet you must apply the Normal format to the paragraph.

1 Select the paragraphs you want to remove bullets from.

2 Choose the Format Paragraph command.

3 Select the Quick Formats tab.

4 Select the Normal radio button and then choose OK.

∴ Indents and Alignment

Calculating Formulas

Works automatically calculates formulas whenever you make a change to a spreadsheet—unless you tell it not to. Why would you want to do that? One reason might be that you want to enter a series of changes and see the impact of all the changes at once. Another reason might be when you are using a very large spreadsheet and the frequent automatic recalculation is too time-consuming.

∴ Manual Calculation

Capturing Text

Works automatically captures up to 256,000 lines of text during a communications session in a temporary storage area called a buffer. You can copy the buffer contents to the Clipboard and then paste them into another document. When you close the communications document, Works discards the buffer contents.

But there might be times when you want to capture more than 256,000 lines, or you might want to capture only a certain portion of the communications session text to a file. For these cases, Works provides the Capture Text command.

To capture incoming text directly to a file, follow these steps:

1 Choose the Tools Capture Text command, or click the Capture Text tool.

2 When the Capture Text dialog box appears, type a name for the file to hold the text.

3 Choose OK.

4 When you want to stop capturing text, choose the Tools End Capture command, or click the Capture Text tool again.

Sending and Receiving Text Files

Cell

 A cell is simply the area in a spreadsheet or database in list view where a row and a column intersect. It's in cells that you enter **values** or **formulas**.

❖ **Active Cell; Cell Address; Cell Selector**

Cell Address

A cell address describes a specific location, or cell, in a spreadsheet using the column letter and row number. For example, H17 identifies the cell at the intersection of column H and row 17.

❖ **Absolute Cell References; Mixed Cell References; Relative Cell References**

Cell Pointer

❖ **Cell Selector**

Cell Selector

The cell selector is the dark outline that marks the **active cell**—the cell where the text, numbers, or formulas you type next are entered. The cell selector is sometimes also called the cell pointer.

Changing Fonts

Works provides two ways to change **fonts**. The quick and easy way is to use the **toolbar**. But if you want to change the font's display color, or select special styles like superscript, subscript, or strikethrough, you need the deluxe tour with the Format Font and Style command.

continues

Changing Fonts *(continued)*

Quick and Easy with the Toolbar

1 To change the font for text you've already typed, first select the text. To change the font for new text, place the **insertion point** where you will type the new text.

2 Click the arrow next to the toolbar's font list box and select the font you want from the list that appears.

3 If you want to change the font's point size, click the arrow next to the toolbar's point-size list box and select the point size you want from the list that appears.

Deluxe Tour with Format Font and Style

1 To change the font for text you've already typed, first select the text. To change the font for new text, place the insertion point where you will type the new text.

2 Choose the Format Font And Style command.

3 When the Font And Style dialog box appears, select the font and the options you want.

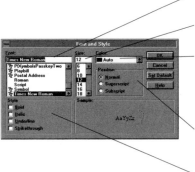

Select a font from the Font list box.

Select a point size from the Size list box.

Select a display color for the text. ("Auto" uses the color for window text set with the Windows Control Panel.)

Choose a position: normal, super^{script}, or sub$_{script}$.

Choose the styles you want: **bold**, *italic*, underline, ~~strikethrough~~, a ***combination***, or none.

4 When you're finished with your selections, choose OK.

Fonts in charts

Changing fonts in **charts** works the same way as in other documents—with one small trick. Works treats all the text in a chart as belonging to one of two groups: the chart title, or everything else. You can change fonts for either one of these groups, but not for individual text items in the chart. To change the chart title font, double-click it and make your font selection. To change the font for everything else, be sure the chart title is not selected and then make your font selection.

 TrueType

Chart Formatting

Works provides several ways to make your charts easier on the eyes. You can change your chart's axes, borders, colors and patterns, gridlines, and markers.

Adding or Removing a Chart Axis

To add or remove a chart's horizontal or left vertical axis, follow these steps:

1 Display the chart and choose the Format Horizontal (X) Axis command or Format Vertical (Y) Axis command.

2 When the Horizontal Axis or Vertical Axis dialog box appears, clear the No Horizontal Axis or No Vertical Axis check box to add the axis, or mark the check box to remove the axis.

3 Choose OK.

To add or remove a right vertical axis, follow these steps:

1 Display the chart and choose the Format Two Vertical (Y) Axes command.

2 When the Two Vertical Axes dialog box appears, choose the Right radio button for at least one series to add a right axis, or choose the Left radio button for all series to remove the right axis.

3 Choose OK.

continues

Chart Formatting *(continued)*

Adding or Removing Chart Borders

To add a border around a chart, display the chart and choose the Format Add Border command. To remove the border, choose Format Add Border again.

Changing Chart Colors and Patterns

To change the colors in a chart, follow these steps:

1 Display the chart and choose the Format Patterns And Colors command.

2 When the Patterns And Colors dialog box appears, select the series (or slice, for a pie chart) you want to format.

3 Select the color you want. Select Auto to have Works choose the colors for you.

4 Select the pattern you want. Select Auto to have Works choose the patterns for you.

5 Choose Format. Or choose Format All to apply your selections to all series.

6 Choose Close.

Colors on a black-and-white printer?

No, Works can't print in color on your black-and-white printer. But it will let you see how your color and pattern selections will appear when printed in black and white. Choose the View Display As Printed command after you make color and pattern choices. If you choose this command before using the Format Pattern And Colors command, only black-and-white color choices appear in the Pattern And Colors dialog box. To see all the colors your monitor can display, choose View Display As Printed again to turn off this option.

Adding or Removing Chart Gridlines

To add or remove gridlines on a chart, follow these steps:

1 Display the chart and choose the Format Horizontal (X) Axis command to add a horizontal grid, or choose the Format Vertical (Y) Axis command to add a vertical grid.

2 When the Horizontal Axis or Vertical Axis dialog box appears, mark the Show Gridlines check box to add gridlines, or clear the check box to remove gridlines.

3 Choose OK.

Changing Chart Markers

To change the markers on a line, x-y scatter, or radar chart, follow these steps:

1 Display the chart and choose Format Patterns And Colors.

2 When the Patterns And Colors dialog box appears, select the series whose markers you want to change.

3 Select the marker shape you want in the Markers box. Select Auto to have Works choose the marker shape for you. Select None to remove markers for the selected series.

4 Choose Format to change the markers for the selected series, or choose Format All to format all series with the selected marker.

5 Choose Close.

Charts

With Works, you can create many different kinds of charts using the data in a spreadsheet. You can save and print the chart by itself, or you can insert it into a word processing document or database **form**.

Creating a Chart

1 Open the spreadsheet containing the data you want to chart, or open a new spreadsheet document and enter the values to be charted.

2 Select the values you want to chart.

3 Choose the Tools Create New Chart command or click the New Chart tool.

4 When the New Chart dialog box appears, choose how you want your chart to look. As you make your selections, the sample chart in the dialog box changes to show how the chart will look with your data.

continues

C

Charts *(continued)*

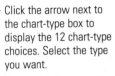

Click the arrow next to the chart-type box to display the 12 chart-type choices. Select the type you want.

Type a title for your chart in the Chart Title box, if you want one.

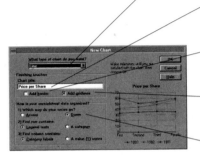

Mark the Add border check box to add a border around the chart.

Mark the Add Gridlines option to show gridlines on the chart.

Answer the three questions about your data by selecting the appropriate radio buttons:
1) Select Across to chart each spreadsheet *row* as a separate group, or choose Down to chart each spreadsheet *column* as a separate group.
2) Select Legend Texts if the first item in each data group is a description of the group, or select A Category if the first item is a value to be charted.
3) Select Category Labels if the first data group contains labels for the x-axis, or select A Value (Y) Series if the first group contains values to be charted.

5 When you're satisfied with the way the sample chart looks, choose OK.

What's a series?

A series is simply chart-talk for a group of values that you want to chart. Pie charts have just one series—whatever you are charting. Other chart types have two or more series. For example, if you are charting your waistline for the last 12 months (not a good application for a pie chart!), your chart has two series—the months that run along the horizontal x-axis (called an x-series or category series), and your measurements that are plotted using the vertical y-axis (called a y-series or value series).

Creating a Chart in a Word Processing Document or Database Form

To create a chart from within a word processing document or database form, follow these steps:

1 Choose the Insert Chart command.

2 When the Insert Chart dialog box appears, select New Chart and choose OK.

3 Works displays a reminder telling you to enter the values to be charted in the spreadsheet. Choose OK.

4 Works embeds an empty spreadsheet directly in your document. Enter the values you want to chart.

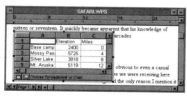

5 Select the values in the spreadsheet you want to chart.

Name that chart

Works saves up to eight charts with each spreadsheet automatically. But it gives them mundane names like Chart1, Chart2, and so on. To name your chart so you can find it more easily, choose the Tools Name Chart command. In the Name Chart dialog box, highlight your chart, type a name in the Name box, and choose Rename.

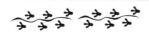

continues

Charts *(continued)*

6 Click the Chart button in the lower left corner of the spreadsheet pane.

7 Works displays the New Chart dialog box. Follow the steps above under "Creating a Chart" to select the chart options you want.

8 Choose OK. Works displays the chart. To continue working on your word processing document or database form, click anywhere outside the chart.

To change the values the chart is based on, double-click the chart in your document or form and then click the Spreadsheet button at the bottom of the chart pane. When the spreadsheet appears, make the changes you want and click the Chart button. Click outside the chart to return to your document or form.

Adding an Existing Chart to a Word Processing Document or to a Database Form

When you add a chart to a word processing document or to a database form, the chart can be linked or unlinked. A linked chart automatically updates whenever the spreadsheet it is based on changes. If you do not want the chart to update after you add it, you want an unlinked chart.

To add a chart, follow these steps:

1 Open the spreadsheet that contains the chart you want to add and display the chart.

2 Open the word processing document or database form that you want to add the chart to.

3 Choose the Window Tile command or use your mouse to arrange the windows so you can see both the chart and the document or form.

4 Drag the chart to the place in your document or form where you want it.

5 When the dialog box appears asking if you want to link the copied data, choose Yes if you want the chart in your document or form to update automatically whenever its spreadsheet changes, or choose No if you don't want the chart to update automatically.

To link or not to link

Linking is a powerful feature that keeps imported charts in sync with their roots. But linking has one other advantage you should know about. When you resize a linked chart, its chart titles, legends, and labels change size automatically with the chart. When you resize an unlinked chart, you must change the size of titles, legends and labels separately, as described in **Changing Fonts**.

> **Chart Formatting; Chart Text; Chart Types; Object Linking and Embedding**

Chart Text

Most charts are more useful if you add some text to identify their different parts. Works does not allow you to add text to a chart by typing directly on the chart. But you can add titles, a legend, labels for the horizontal axis (category labels), and labels for each plotted value (data labels).

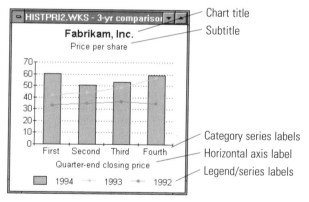

continues

Chart Text *(continued)*

Chart Titles

Chart titles identify the chart itself and its key elements. You can add a main chart title, a subtitle, and titles for the vertical and horizontal axes. To add a title, follow these steps:

1 With the chart displayed, choose the Edit Titles command.

2 When the Titles dialog box appears, type the title you want (or a reference to a spreadsheet cell containing the title) in the appropriate box.

3 Choose OK.

To change or delete a title, follow the same steps and make the changes or deletions you want in the Titles dialog box.

Chart Legends

A chart legend is a set of labels that identify the series of values plotted in the chart. When you create an area, bar, or line chart, Works automatically adds a legend for you at the bottom of the chart. If the spreadsheet rows or columns that the chart is based on include titles, Works uses those titles for the legend. Otherwise, Works supplies the series labels Series 1, Series 2, and so on.

To add a chart legend, follow these steps:

1 With the chart displayed, choose the Edit Legend/Series Labels command.

2 When the Legend/Series Label dialog box appears, make sure the Auto Series Label check box is not marked. If it is marked, Works uses its built-in Series 1, Series 2 labels.

3 Type the name you want (or a reference to a spreadsheet cell containing the name) for each series in your chart.

4 If the chart is an area chart, and you want the series labels inside the charted areas rather than as a legend at the bottom of the chart, select Use As Area Labels.

5 Choose OK.

To change or delete a legend, follow the same steps and make the changes or deletions you want in the Legend/Series Label dialog box.

C

Chart Labels for Pie Charts

Pie chart slices can have two labels each. For each label, you can select from five different label types:

Label type	What it shows
Values	The values used to plot the slices
Percentages	The percentage of the total each slice represents
Cell contents	The contents of any cell range you specify
1, 2, 3, ...	Sequential numbers for each slice
None	No label

To add labels to a pie chart, follow these steps:

1 With the pie chart displayed, choose the Edit Data Labels command.

2 When the Data Labels dialog box appears, choose the labels you want. If you choose Cell contents, enter the spreadsheet cell range containing the labels you want in the Cell Range box.

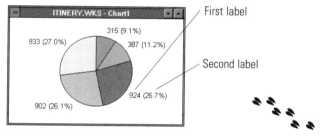

First label

Second label

3 Choose OK.

To change labels for a pie chart, follow the same steps and make the changes you want in the Data Labels dialog box. To delete labels completely, select the None option for both labels.

Chart Labels for Other Charts

To add labels to area, bar, line, or radar charts, you enter the labels into the spreadsheet the chart is based on, and then copy and paste them into place in the chart. You can paste the labels along the horizontal axis (called category labels), or you can paste the labels into the body of the chart (called value or data labels).

continues

Chart Text *(continued)*

To add labels to a chart other than a pie chart, follow these steps:

1 In the spreadsheet the chart is based on, enter the text or numbers you want for the labels. (To access the spreadsheet for a chart embedded in another document, double-click the chart and then choose View Spreadsheet.)

2 Select the cells containing the label text or numbers.

3 Choose the Edit Copy command.

4 Choose the View Chart command to switch to the chart you want to label.

5 Choose the Edit Series command.

6 When the Series dialog box appears, move the insertion point to the Category (X) Series box to add the labels to the horizontal axis.

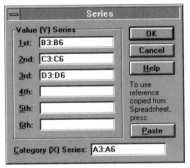

7 Choose the Paste button.

8 Choose OK.

To change labels, follow the same steps and paste the new labels in the Series dialog box. To delete labels, choose the Edit Series command and make the deletions you want in the Series dialog box.

Chart Types
Works provides 12 different types of charts for you to choose from: area charts, bar charts, line charts, pie charts, stacked line charts, x-y scatter charts, radar charts, combination charts, 3-D area charts, 3-D bar charts, 3-D line charts, and 3-D pie charts. Works shows you examples of each of these chart types when you create a new chart, or when you change the type for an existing chart.

Choosing a Chart Type for a New Chart

When you create a chart, Works presents a list of chart types in its New Chart dialog box.

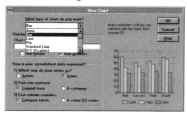

You can see what your data will look like in each chart type by selecting different types in the New Chart dialog box. Each time you select a chart type, Works shows you a sample chart using your data.

Changing the Chart Type for an Existing Chart

To change the type for an existing chart, follow these steps:

1 Open the spreadsheet that the chart is based on. (To change the type for a chart embedded in another document, double-click the chart and skip to step 4.)

2 Choose the View Chart command.

3 When the Charts dialog box appears, select the chart you want to change and choose OK.

4 Open the Gallery menu and choose the type of chart you want or click the tool for the chart type you want.

5 Works presents a dialog box with up to six varieties of charts for you to choose. Simply click the variety you want.

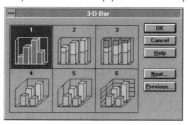

Next, please

If you choose a chart type and decide you don't like any of the varieties you see in the dialog box, choose Next or Previous to see the varieties for another chart type. You can use these buttons to quickly view the available varieties for all 12 chart types.

Circular Reference

See *Reference, Circular*. (Just kidding!) If you see the message CIRC in the **status bar** when entering **formulas** in a spreadsheet, you've fallen into the circular reference trap: The formula in one cell uses a **value** in a second cell, but the formula in the second cell uses a value from the first cell—something like, cell B1 contains =10*C1, and cell C1 contains =10*B1. To get out of the trap, simply change one of the formulas.

Dependents; Precedents

ClipArt Gallery

Works comes with a collection of pictures, or clip art, you can insert into your word processing documents and database **forms**.

Viewing the ClipArt Gallery

To see the pictures in the gallery, choose the Insert ClipArt command.

The ClipArt Gallery organizes the available pictures into categories as shown in the list box at the top of the dialog box. You can select the category you want to see or you can select All Categories to view all pictures.

Maintaining the ClipArt Gallery

You can do several things to keep the ClipArt Gallery organized and up-to-date. To use the gallery maintenance options, choose the Options button in the ClipArt Gallery dialog box.

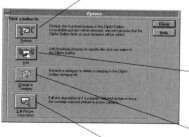

Choose Refresh to update the ClipArt Gallery to reflect any additions, changes, or deletions you made to pictures stored on your computer. Choose Refresh also to locate pictures on your computer that you might want to add to the gallery.

Choose Add to add a specific picture or collection to the ClipArt Gallery.

Choose Change A Category to change the name of a category, or to delete a category.

Choose Edit Picture Information to move a picture from one category to another, or to change the description of the image.

 Adding Pictures

Clipboard The Clipboard is a temporary holding area. It is a feature in Windows that lets you move information between one part of a document and another part, between one Works document and another, or between Works and another Windows-based program. You use the Clipboard whenever you use the Edit Cut or Edit Copy commands. Works stores the text or picture you cut or copy on the Clipboard temporarily until you decide to insert it somewhere with the Edit Paste command.

continues

Clipboard *(continued)*

Two important things to remember about the Clipboard:

- It holds only one item at a time. Each time you use Edit Cut or Edit Copy to put something on the Clipboard, you replace whatever was previously on the Clipboard.

- It is temporary. When you turn off your computer or exit Windows, the contents of the Clipboard are lost.

∴ **Object Linking and Embedding**

Closing Documents
To close a Works document, choose the File Close command. If you've made changes to the document since you last saved it, Works asks if you want to save the document.

Color
You can change the color of most parts of Works documents.

Coloring database forms—**Shading**
Coloring spreadsheet cells—**Shading**
Coloring text—**Changing Fonts**
Coloring borders—**Borders**
Changing chart colors—**Chart Formatting**

Columns
In a spreadsheet each column (a single vertical line of **cells**) is identified by a letter, which appears at the top of the column. In **list view,** every database **field** occupies a column. You can apply anything you know about spreadsheet columns (such as how to adjust the **column width** or select columns) to fields.

∴ **Inserting Columns and Rows; Selecting Columns and Rows; Text Columns**

C

Column Width You can change the width of a column with the mouse or with the Format Column Width command.

Drag the edge of the column letter to change the width of that column.

The perfect column width

To adjust the column width to fit the widest entry in the column, double-click the column letter or mark the Best Fit check box in the Column Width dialog box.

Communication Settings Before you can communicate with another computer, you need to tell Works how to talk to the other computer. You do so by choosing the Settings Communication command.

When the Settings dialog box appears, it contains the most common settings already filled in as suggestions. Works is pretty good at detecting your computer's needs, so you most likely will not have to change these settings.

continues

Communication Settings *(continued)*

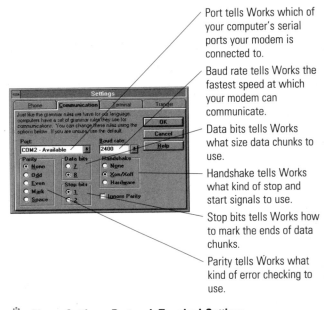

Port tells Works which of your computer's serial ports your modem is connected to.

Baud rate tells Works the fastest speed at which your modem can communicate.

Data bits tells Works what size data chunks to use.

Handshake tells Works what kind of stop and start signals to use.

Stop bits tells Works how to mark the ends of data chunks.

Parity tells Works what kind of error checking to use.

∴ **Phone Settings; Protocol; Terminal Settings**

Comparing Values

∴ **Formulas; Functions**

COM Ports A COM port, also known as a serial port, is a connection where an accessory, such as a modem, a mouse, or a serial printer, can be attached to your computer. Computers can have up to four COM ports, called COM 1, COM 2, COM 3, and COM 4.

∴ **Communication Settings; Modem Setup**

C

Control-Menu Commands

The Control menu is the menu that appears when you click the small hyphen in the upper left corner of a window or **dialog box**. It contains a number of handy commands that let you manipulate Works windows and dialog boxes. Not all commands appear on all Control menus—dialog-box Control menus usually contain only Move and Close commands, for example—but here's a complete list:

Command	What it does
Restore	Returns the window to its previous size
Move	Lets you use the direction keys to move the window or dialog box around the screen
Size	Lets you use the direction keys to change the size of the window
Minimize	Shrinks the window to an icon (To restore a minimized window, click the icon to display its Control menu.)
Maximize	Expands the window to its fullest size
Close	Closes the window or dialog box (When you close an **application window**, all the **document windows** it contains close as well.)
Switch To	Displays the Windows Task List, from which you can manage all the open application windows on your desktop

Converting Files

∴ **Exporting Documents; Opening Documents**

C

Copying The easiest way to copy text, pictures, **charts, cells,** or **ranges** in Works is with **drag-and-drop**.

Copying from One Window to Another

Using drag-and-drop, you can copy information to another similar Works document, a different kind of Works document, or to any document created in a Windows-based application.

1 Open both documents and arrange them so you can see them both.

2 Select the information you want to copy and drag it to another window.

Copying Within the Same Window

To copy information from one place to another within the same document, hold down Ctrl while you drag. Otherwise, Works thinks you want to move the selection and cuts the information from its old location.

Clipboard

Copying Data You can copy data within a **database** the same way you copy text in a word processor document: You hold down Ctrl as you **drag-and-drop**, or use Edit Copy and Edit Paste.

But did you know you can copy data from a database to another Works database, a Works spreadsheet, or a Works word processor document? You use the same technique:

1 Open the source and destination documents and arrange the windows so both are visible.

2 Select the data you want to copy.

3 Point to the border of the selected data, and then drag it to another window.

When you drag database information to a word processor document, each **field** is separated by a tab character, and each **record** ends with a paragraph mark.

When you drag to a spreadsheet, each field becomes a **column** and each record becomes a **row**; the spreadsheet looks much like database **list view**.

You can also drag information to many other Windows-based applications. Which ones? Try it!

Nonprinting Characters

Copying Formatting  To copy just the style or format of text without copying the text itself, follow these steps:

1 Select the text whose style or format you want.

2 Choose the Edit Copy command.

3 Select the character or paragraph you want to copy the formatting to.

4 Choose the Edit Paste Special command.

5 In the Paste Special dialog box, select Character Style or Paragraph Format.

6 Choose OK.

Copying Formulas To copy **formulas** (or any other cell contents) in a spreadsheet, follow these steps:

1 Select the cells containing the formulas you want to copy.

2 Point to the border of the selected cells, and then drag the selection to another window. Or, to copy the selected cells to another location within the same spreadsheet, hold down Ctrl and drag the selection.

Copying Values; Filling Cells

Copying Objects and Pictures

You can copy objects (such as **Note-It** notes, **tables**, and **charts**) and pictures within a document by selecting the object, holding down Ctrl, and dragging the object where you want it.

Alternatively, you can use the Edit Copy and Edit Paste commands.

> **Drag-and-Drop; Moving Objects and Pictures; Selecting Objects**

Copying Text

The easiest way to copy selected text is to hold down Ctrl and drag the object to the desired location.

You can also copy text by following these steps:

1 Select the text you want to copy.

2 Choose the Edit Copy command, which places a copy of the text on the **Clipboard**.

3 Place the **insertion point** where you want the text.

4 Choose the Edit Paste command.

> **Drag-and-Drop; Moving Text; Selecting Text**

Copying Values

To copy **values** without copying the actual **formulas** that produce the values, follow these steps:

1 Select the cell or range that contains the formulas.

2 Choose the Edit Copy command.

3 Move the **cell selector** where you want to insert the values.

4 Choose the Edit Paste Special command.

5 When the Paste Special dialog box appears, select the Values only radio button.

6 Choose OK.

> **Copying Formulas**

Counting Words ✍ To count the number of words in a document, choose the Tools Word Count command. To count the words in a portion of a document, select the portion you want to count before choosing the Tools Word Count command.

Cue Cards ✍ 🖥 🖥 🖥 Cue Cards are the Works version of the TelePrompTer. They stay on top of your document window to give you step-by-step instructions on basic Works tasks. To turn on Cue Cards, choose the Help Cue Cards command. To turn off Cue Cards, choose the Help Cue Cards command again.

Currency Symbols 🖥 🖥 Works uses a currency symbol, usually a dollar sign, for **values** you format as currency. But if you're the worldly type, you might want Works to use a different currency symbol, like £ or ¥. To change the currency symbol, follow these steps:

1 From Program Manager, start the Windows Control Panel (in the Main program group).

2 Double-click the International icon.

3 Choose the Change button in the Currency Format box.

continues

Currency Symbols *(continued)*

4 Enter the currency symbol you want in the Symbol text box. (If the symbol isn't on your keyboard, enter it as an **ANSI character**.)

5 Choose OK two times to close the International dialog box. Your new settings take effect immediately.

⋮ **Formatting Numbers**

Customizing Toolbars
Each Works module has its own **toolbar**, and you can customize each toolbar to fit the way you work by adding special tools you use and by removing standard tools you don't use.

To customize a toolbar, choose the Tools Customize Toolbar command or double-click any blank space on the toolbar to open the Customize Works Toolbar dialog box.

To remove a tool from the toolbar, drag the tool anywhere off the toolbar.

To add a tool to the toolbar, select the category of the button you want to add from the list in the Categories box.

Then drag the button you want to add to its new location on the toolbar.

To move a tool to a different position on the toolbar, drag the tool to its new location.

To reset the toolbar to its original configuration, choose the Reset button.

When you've got the toolbar the way you want it, choose OK.

⋮ Quick Reference contains a complete list of available toolbar buttons.

D

Cutting

 When you cut information, you remove it from its place in your document, spreadsheet, or database form, and place it temporarily on the **Clipboard**—usually in preparation to move it somewhere else by **pasting** it.

To cut information, select it and then choose the Edit Cut command, press Ctrl+X, or click the Cut tool.

Data Markers

 **Chart Formatting**

Databases

A database is a Works document you use to organize and access information. What kinds of information? Your address book, a mailing list, recipes, business contact list, a home inventory, an audio, video, or book collection—in short, anything you might keep track of with a Rolodex or index cards—is a great candidate for a database.

Creating Databases

The easiest way to create a database is to use a **WorksWizard**.

1 Choose the File WorksWizards command, or choose the Use A WorksWizard button from the Works Startup dialog.

2 Select an application closest to what you want from the WorksWizards list or select Quick Database for a general purpose database. (You can customize the database after the WorksWizard creates it.)

3 Choose OK.

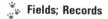 **Fields; Records**

Date and Time Functions Works has nine func-
tions that make working with dates and times in spreadsheets and databases easier. For example, you can use the
DAY(), MONTH(), or YEAR() function to extract the
day of the month, month, or year from a particular date.
An especially handy date function is the NOW() function.
Put this **formula** in your spreadsheet, and it will always
display the correct current date:

=NOW()

❖ **Arguments**

Date Formats  Works gives you several different ways
to format dates in your spreadsheets and databases. To set
or change a date format, select the cell or field containing
the date, and then choose the Format Number command.
Select the Date radio button and select the format you
want from the list.

❖ **Formatting Numbers**

dBASE  dBASE is a database program that's been around
since the dawn of civilization—well, since the dawn of
personal computers anyway. You can exchange documents with users of dBASE III or dBASE IV because
Works can open and save documents in those formats.

❖ **Exporting Documents; Opening Documents; Saving
Documents**

D

Deleting Columns and Rows To delete or remove
columns or rows from a spreadsheet, select the columns
or rows and then choose the Insert Delete Row/Column
command.

To delete or clear column or row contents without
removing the column or row itself, select the column or
row and then press the Del key.

Erasing Cells

Deleting Fields To delete or remove fields from a data-
base, select the fields and then choose the Insert Delete
Selection command in **form view**, or the Insert Delete
Record/Field command in **list view**.

To delete or clear field contents without removing the
field itself, select the field and choose the Edit Clear Field
Entry command.

Deleting Files Works saves all of your docu-
ments and forms on disk as files. To delete a file, you can
use either Windows File Manager or the **File Organizer
WorksWizard**. For information on using File Manager,
check your Windows user's manual.

Deleting Objects To delete objects (such as pictures,
Note-It notes, **tables**, and **charts**), click the object to select it and press the Del key.

Deleting Records

To delete a record in **list view**, click the row number to select the record and choose the Insert Delete Record/Field command. To delete a record in **form view**, display the record and choose the Insert Delete Record command.

∴ **Hiding Records**

Deleting Text

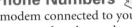 To delete text, select the text and press the Del key.

Dependents

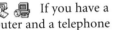 A dependent **cell** is one containing a **formula** that references another cell. For example, if cell A5 contains the formula =A3+A4, then cell A5 is dependent; it depends on obtaining values from cells A3 and A4 before it can calculate properly.

∴ **ERR Message; Precedents**

Dialing Phone Numbers

If you have a modem connected to your computer and a telephone connected to the modem, you can use Works to dial the phone for you. Simply select the number you want to dial in a word processor document, database, or spreadsheet, and then choose the Tools Dial This Number command. Your modem dials the number, and then you can pick up the telephone handset.

In the communications module, you can dial the number in the **phone settings** dialog box by clicking the Dial tool or choosing the Phone Dial command.

∴ **Modem Setup**

Dialog Box

A dialog box is a mini-window that Works displays when it needs some information from you. A typical dialog box has several options for you to choose.

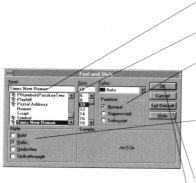

Select an item from a list.

Click the arrows to scroll the list.

Click a radio button to choose an option. Click another button to choose a different option.

Mark one or more check boxes to select options. Clear its check box to turn an option off.

Choose Help for online help with the options in the dialog box.

Choose OK when you're satisfied with your selections.

Documents

A Works document is what you see when you open a file. It can be a word processor document, a spreadsheet document, a database document, or a communications document. You can open up to eight documents at one time, each within its own window.

Document Views

 Views

Document Window A document window is a window that holds an open **document**. Just as an **application window** is fully contained within your computer's display screen, a document window is fully contained within its application window. You can have up to eight document windows open at a time in Works.

* **Control-Menu Commands**

Drag-and-Drop Drag-and-drop is a technique that lets you move or copy parts of a document using the mouse.

Moving with Drag-and-Drop

To move part of a document, select it and then drag it to its new location. (By drag, I mean click the mouse button and hold it down while you move the mouse pointer to the destination. The "drop" part comes in when you let go of the button.) To drag cells in a spreadsheet or in database list view, you must point to the selected cells' border before you click.

Copying with Drag-and-Drop

The technique for copying part of another document is exactly the same as for moving (described above), except you hold down the Ctrl key while you drag.

Draw Draw is the Microsoft tool that lets you create or modify drawings that you can insert into a word processor document or database **form**.

Creating or Changing a Drawing

To create a drawing, choose the Insert Drawing command. To change a drawing, double-click the drawing. When the Draw window appears, choose the tool you need from the Draw toolbar.

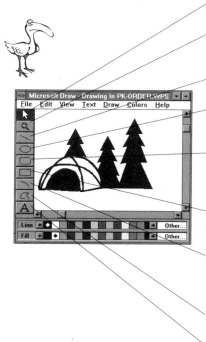

Use to select and move objects.

Click to zoom in on an object for a closer view. Shift+click to zoom out.

Drag to draw a straight line.

Drag to draw an ellipse. Shift+drag to draw a perfect circle.

Drag to draw a rectangle with rounded corners. Shift+drag to draw a rounded square.

Drag to draw a rectangle. Shift+drag to draw a square.

Drag to draw an arc. Choose the Draw Filled command and drag to draw a pie slice.

Drag to draw freehand forms.

Click and then type up to 255 characters.

Adding a Drawing to a Document

To add a drawing you create with Microsoft Draw to your word processing or database document, follow these steps:

1 From the Microsoft Draw window, choose the File Exit And Return command.

2 Works asks if you want to update the document. Choose Yes to return to Works and add the drawing.

3 Works inserts the drawing at the insertion point.

Easy Connect

The Easy Connect dialog box lists your eight most recent communication connections, and lets you easily reconnect to one of them or define a new connection. The Easy Connect dialog box appears when you choose the File Create New File command and then click the Communications button or, more simply, choose the Phone Easy Connect command when a communications document is already open and active.

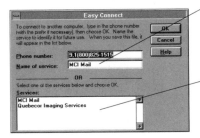

Type the phone number (including prefix) and the name of the service to connect to a service for the first time.

Or select the name of a service from the list to reestablish a previous connection.

☙ **New Documents; Phone Settings; Communication Settings; Modem Setup**

Editing Cells

To replace the contents of a **cell**, select the cell and begin typing. Notice that as you type, your new entry appears in two places: in the **active cell** and in the **formula bar**. If you want to move the **insertion point** within your new entry—or if you want to make minor changes to an existing entry—press F2 or click the formula bar where you want the insertion point.

When the formula bar contains the text, **value**, or **formula** that you want to appear in the cell, press Enter or click the formula bar's check-mark button. If you change your mind and decide not to change the cell's contents, press Esc or click the formula bar's × button.

E

Faster editing of multiple cells

If you are going to make entries in several cells, select them all before you begin making entries. When multiple cells are selected, Works automatically makes the next cell in the selection the active cell when you press Enter or click the check-mark button.

Erasing Cells; Functions; Selecting Cells

Editing Charts

To change a **chart** that you've already created, begin by double-clicking the chart. (In the spreadsheet module, choose the View Chart command.) The menus change to indicate that the charting module is active. You can then change the **chart type** (Gallery menu), add or delete chart titles, edit the data in the chart—in fact, do anything you can when you create a new chart.

Chart Formatting

Editing Records

You can edit **records** in a **database** in either **form view** or **list view**. The procedure for editing data items is exactly the same as the procedure for **editing cells.**

Adding Records; Deleting Records

Editing Text

To edit text that you've already entered, select the text that you want to change. Then type; the new text you type replaces the selection. If you want to add new text without replacing existing text, position the **insertion point** and begin typing.

Entering Text; Selecting Text

E

Embedding and Linking Existing Objects

To create an object from an existing file (a Works document or a file from another application), follow these steps:

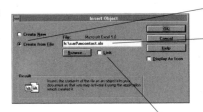

1 Place the **insertion point** where you want the object.

2 Choose the Insert Object command.

3 Select the Create From File radio button.

4 Type the name of the file in the File text box. If you're not sure of the name—or you're a lousy typist—choose the Browse button and select the filename from the list that appears.

5 If you want to link the object (so that any time you make a change in the original file, your Works document gets updated), mark the Link check box.

6 Choose OK.

 The easiest way

To insert a **range** or **chart** from an open Works spreadsheet into a word processor document or database **form**, choose the Insert Spreadsheet/Table or Insert Chart command. Works displays a dialog box that lists the open spreadsheets and their named ranges or charts; simply select the one you want to insert.

 Drag-and-Drop; Object Linking and Embedding

Embedding New Objects  To create a new object

from an application other than Microsoft Works and embed it in a Works word processor document or database
form, follow these steps:

1 Place the **insertion point** where you want the object.

2 Choose the Insert Object command.

3 Select the Create New radio button.

4 Select the type of object you want to embed.

5 Choose OK. Works starts the application associated with the selected object type, allowing you to create the object.

∴ **Object Linking and Embedding**

Ending Lines  Thanks to **word wrap,** you normally don't

have to worry about line endings; they just happen. If you
want to end a line without ending a **paragraph**, press
Shift+Enter.

Endnotes

Endnotes, like **footnotes**, are used for documenting quotations or for making incidental comments that you don't want to include in the main text. Endnotes, however, appear at the end of the document instead of at the bottom of the page where the reference occurs. If that's what you want, follow these steps:

1 Create your footnotes in the usual way. (See **Footnotes**.)

2 Choose the File Page Setup command and select the Other Options tab.

3 Mark the Print Footnotes At End Of Document check box.

Entering Data

You can enter data—text, numbers, or **formulas**—into a database in either **list view** or **form view**.

Entering Text or Numbers

Select the **field** where you want to enter data and then type. Press Tab to move to the next field. Pressing Tab in the last field of a **record** moves the highlight to the first field of the next record.

Entering Formulas

You enter formulas just like text or numbers—except you must begin the entry with an equal sign (=). To calculate the selling price for an inventory item in a field, for example, you might enter this formula:

=Cost*1.5

Works displays the formula in the **formula bar**, and the result of the formula in the field. Works automatically enters the formula in every record in the database.

E

Proposing default entries

You can use a formula to automatically enter information that is the same for most records in a database. For example, if most members of your photography club live in California, put the formula ="CA" in the State field. Works proposes CA as the entry for each new record. But if you have a member who moved to Nevada (probably to avoid taxes), just type *NV* when you enter her record.

Entering Numbers To enter information such as numeric **values, formulas**, or labels in a spreadsheet, click the **cell** where you want the information and then type.

✦ Filling Cells; Fill Series; Formula Bar

Entering Text 🖎 🖳 To enter text in a word processor document, just type away. Were you expecting this to be difficult?

Don't press Enter (except at the end of a paragraph)

When you reach the right margin, keep typing. (Don't press Enter.) Works moves the **insertion point** to the next line automatically. This feature is called **word wrap**, and you'll really come to appreciate it if you later make changes to your text, because the line endings will automatically change as needed.

Entering Text on a Database Form

You can place text anywhere on a database **form** by following these steps:

1 Be sure the form is not protected against changes. Choose the Format Protection command and clear the Protect Form check box.

2 Place the **insertion point** where you want to add text.

3 Type your text and press Enter when you're done. (Don't end your text with a colon, because then the text becomes the name of a new field. If that's what you want, see **Adding Fields** for more information.)

✦ Ending Lines; Entering Data; Protecting Form Designs

Envelopes To create an envelope, choose the Tools Envelopes And Labels command and select the Envelopes tab.

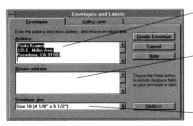

1 Type the recipient's address in the Address text box.

2 Type your return address if you want it printed on the envelope.

3 Select the envelope size.

4 Click Create Envelope, and Works inserts the envelope text at the beginning of your document.

5 To print the envelope, choose the File Print command and select the Envelope radio button.

Select the address first

Select the text that you want in the Address text box before you choose the Tools Envelopes And Labels command, and Works automatically inserts it for you.

Mail Merge; Options

Erasing

You can erase (or delete) cells, columns, rows, fields, records, text, objects, and files.

Clearing cell contents—**Erasing Cells**

Removing columns—**Deleting Columns and Rows**

Removing fields—**Deleting Fields**

Removing files—**Deleting Files; File Organizer WorksWizard**

Removing objects—**Deleting Objects**

Removing records—**Deleting Records**

Removing rows—**Deleting Columns and Rows**

Removing text—**Deleting Text**

Erasing Cells

You can erase the contents of one or more **cells**. To do so, select the cells you want to erase and then choose the Edit Clear command or, more simply, press Del.

Erasing a cell does not remove the cell from the spreadsheet or database; it simply clears the cell's contents.

Clearing a formula in a database

Database fields that contain a **formula** act a little differently from other cells. If you want to erase a formula in **list view**, you must select the entire field and then choose the Edit Clear Formula command.

Deleting Columns and Rows; Deleting Fields; Deleting Records; Selecting Cells

ERR Message

If you see a **cell** that contains "ERR," that cell's **formula** has an err. Er, I mean error. This occurs when your formula attempts a mathematically impossible feat, such as dividing by zero or calculating the square root of a negative number.

Cells that are **dependent** on an ERR cell also contain ERR.

To ERR is human

Sometimes you'll *want* the ERR message to appear as a signal that there's an error somewhere in your data. That's easy: Use the ERR() **function**. The following example displays ERR if the value of cell A5 is less than 10; otherwise it displays the value of cell A5:

=IF(A5<10,ERR(),A5)

 Informational Functions

Exiting Works

To exit from Works—or almost any other Windows-based application—you can use any of these techniques:

- Choose the File Exit Works command
- Press Alt+F4
- Double-click the Control-menu box

If you have any open documents that you haven't saved, Works asks if you want to save them before quitting.

 Closing Documents; Control-Menu Commands; Saving Documents

Exporting Documents

Exporting is the process of saving a file in a format that you can use with another program. You might find this ability useful if you use Works on a portable computer and Microsoft Word and Excel on your desktop computer, for example.

To export a document, choose the File Save As command, and then select a format that your other program can open.

You can export this file type	From these modules
Comma-separated text	
dBASE III	
dBASE IV	
Lotus 1-2-3 version 2.x	
Microsoft Excel versions 4.0 and 5.0	
Microsoft Windows Write	
Microsoft Word for Windows versions 2.0 and 6.0	
Microsoft Works for Macintosh version 3.0	
Microsoft Works for MS-DOS	
Microsoft Works for Windows versions 1.0 and 2.0	
Tab-separated text	
Text	
WordPerfect version 5.x	

Works can also import (open) files saved in each of these formats; see **Opening Documents**.

> **ASCII Text Files; dBASE; Lotus 1-2-3; Microsoft Excel; Microsoft Word; Sharing Works Data; WordPerfect; Write**

Field Lines

Field lines are the dotted lines that indicate the **field** locations in the database **form view**. You can make them appear and disappear by choosing the View Field Lines command.

Printing field lines

The setting of the View Field Lines command does not control whether field lines print when you print a form. To control that feature, choose the File Page Setup command, select the Other Options tab, and use the Print Field Lines check box.

Field Names

Every **field** in a **database** must have a name by which you can identify it. Works imposes only a couple restrictions in naming a field: The name cannot be longer than 15 characters, and it can't start with an apostrophe. If you don't specify a name when you create a new field, Works assigns a nondescriptive name like "Field 17."

Hiding a Field Name in Form View

In **form view**, the field name (followed by a colon) appears to the left of each field. If you don't want to see the name (you might want to replace it with something more descriptive), select the field and then choose the Format Show Field Name command.

Fields

A field is a single piece of information in a **database**, such as Last Name, City, or Price. When you display a database in **list view**, each column is a field; the **field name** is at the top of the document window. In **form view**, each field appears next to its field name.

Adding Fields; Deleting Fields

Filenames

You give a document a name when you choose the File Save or File Save As command. The standard MS-DOS file-naming rules apply:

- A filename can't be longer than eight characters, plus a three-character extension.

- Filenames can contain letters, numbers, and most symbols, but not spaces or the handful of symbols that MS-DOS reserves for other purposes:

  " * + , . / : ; < = > ? [\ ] ¦

Works automatically assigns an appropriate extension for the document. If you export a document for use in another program, Works uses that program's extension; if you save a document in the Works format, Works uses one of the following extensions:

Module	Extension
Word processor	WPS
Spreadsheet	WKS
Database	WDB
Communications	WCM

 **Exporting Documents; Saving Documents**

File Organizer WorksWizard 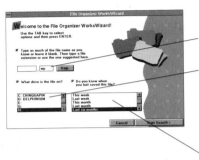 Can't find
a file? Need to delete some files because your disk is full?
The File Organizer **WorksWizard** helps you find files and
lets you view, open, rename, move, copy, or delete them.
To use it, follow these steps:

1 Choose the File
WorksWizards com-
mand. In the Startup
dialog box, select File
Organizer.

2 Type as much of the
filename as you know.

3 Select the drive you
think the file is on. The
File Organizer
WorksWizard searches
all directories on the
drive you select.

4 Select the date range
when the file was last
saved.

5 Choose the Start Search button. Works displays the files that it finds.

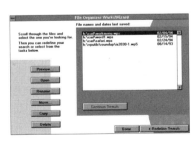

6 Select a file and then choose a button for the action you want. If
the file you're looking for isn't listed, click Redefine Search.

Deleting Files; Opening Documents

Filling Cells You can copy the contents of one or more **cells** into adjacent cells by choosing the Edit Fill Down or Edit Fill Right command. Follow these steps:

1 Highlight the cells you want to copy and the cells where you want the copies to end up.

2 Choose the Edit Fill Down command to copy the contents of the first row of highlighted cells into each of the highlighted cells below, or choose Edit Fill Right to copy the contents of the first column of highlighted cells into each of the highlighted cells to the right.

Updating references

When a cell you copy contains a **relative cell reference**, the reference is adjusted in each of the copies. For example, if cell B10 contains the formula =SUM(B2:B9) and you use Edit Fill Right, cell C10 will contain =SUM(C2:C9).

∴ Copying Data; Copying Formulas; Fill Series; Selecting Cells

---

Fill Series 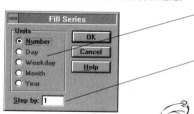 You can fill a range of **cells** with a series of numbers or dates. Use this feature if you want to create a list of even numbers, for example, or list a series of dates, such as every other Friday. Here's how:

1 Enter the series' first value in the cell where you want the series to begin.

2 Select the range of cells where you want the series.

3 Choose the Edit Fill Series command.

4 Select the unit if you're creating a series of dates.

5 Type the interval in the Step By text box.

F.

Filtering Records

> **Finding Records; Queries**

Financial Functions

Works has 11 financial **functions** that can quickly calculate depreciation, investment returns, and so on. Do you want to know what your monthly payment will be on the new Land Rover? Enter this formula, which calculates the payment for a $30,000 loan at 9% annual interest, to be paid off in 60 easy monthly payments:

=PMT(30000,.09/12,60)

This should pique your interest

Avoid a common error: Be sure that the interest rate argument is for the period specified in the period argument. For example, if the period is monthly, use the monthly interest rate—not the annual interest rate. (That's why I divided the 9% annual rate by 12 in the example above.)

> **Arguments**

WORKS A TO Z

F

Finding Cells 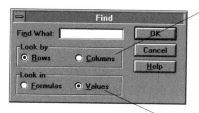 Choose the Edit Find command to locate the next **cell** that contains the information you specify.

Works begins its search in the upper left corner of the selection. Use the Look By radio buttons to specify whether Works should search across the spreadsheet first (mark Rows) or down the spreadsheet (Columns).

Use the Look In radio buttons to tell Works whether to look in each cell's **formula**, or in the **value** produced by the formula.

 **Finding Records**

Finding Files

File Organizer WorksWizard

Finding Records  To quickly and simply find a **record** that contains certain text, choose the Edit Find command. Type the text you're looking for—Works ignores capitalization in its search—and Works selects the next **field** that contains the text.

continues

F

Finding Records *(continued)*

A simple query

You can also use the Edit Find command to view all the records that
contain the text you're looking for. In the Find dialog box, mark All
Records. Works then displays only the records that contain the text you specify,
and hides the rest.

 Hiding Records; Queries

Finding Text

Choose the Edit Find command to locate
phrases, words, or other snippets of text in a word processor document. Before you use the Edit Find command,
select the document area that you want Works to search;
if you want to search the entire document, be sure that no
text is selected.

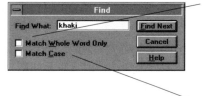

Mark the Match Whole
Word Only check box if
you want Works to ignore
occurrences of the Find
What text that are
contained within a longer
word.

Mark the Match Case
check box if you want
Works to find only text
that matches exactly—
including capitalization.

Finding Special Characters

Besides locating letters, numbers, and punctuation, the Edit Find
command can search for **nonprinting characters** and other funny
symbols.

To search for	Type this in the Find What box
An end-of-line mark	^n
A **paragraph** mark	^p
A **page break**	^d
A tab character	^t
A **nonbreaking space**	^s
White space (tab characters or spaces)	^w
Any character	?
An **ANSI character** (Replace *nnnn* with the numeric code for the character you want to find.)	^*nnnn*
A question mark	^?
A caret (^)	^^

Finding Cells; Finding Records; Selecting Text

Fonts

You can use a variety of fonts (type styles) in your Works documents. Windows 3.1 includes the following fonts, but a visit to any software store or shareware forum will present thousands more:

Arial looks a lot like Helvetica, a popular sans serif font.

`Courier New recalls the days of typewriters.`

Times New Roman is easy to read.

ΙφΨΟΥΔεχοδεΤηισψου ———These characters are from the TrueType Symbol font.

♦≈□◆●♎♏♍♦♒☺♓✗♍——These characters are from the TrueType Wingdings font.

Changing Fonts

Footers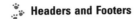

❖ **Headers and Footers**

Footnotes 📝 Footnotes, which appear at the bottom of the page, are used for documenting quotations or for making incidental comments that you don't want to include in the main text.

Adding a Footnote

1 Place the **insertion point** where you want the footnote reference to appear.

2 Choose the Insert Footnote command. Works displays the Footnote dialog box.

3 Select the Numbered radio button if you want Works to number footnotes consecutively, or select Character Mark and enter the character if you want to use a symbol such as an asterisk as the footnote marker.

4 Press Enter. Works opens the footnote pane and places the insertion point there so you can type your footnote text.

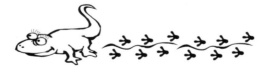

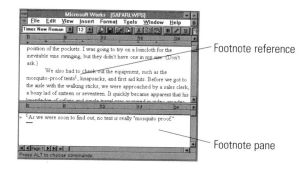

Footnote reference

Footnote pane

Deleting a Footnote

To delete a footnote, select the footnote marker and press Del. The footnote is deleted from the footnote pane, and the remaining footnotes are automatically renumbered.

❖ Endnotes; Window Panes

Formatting
✎ 🖥 🖨 The Bible admonishes, "Judge not according to the appearance" (John 7:24), but judicious formatting sure makes documents easier to read.

continues

Formatting *(continued)*

Adding borders and shading—**Borders; Patterns; Shading**

Changing colors—**Borders; Changing Fonts; Chart Formatting; Shading**

Changing font styles—**Bold Characters; Changing Fonts; Fonts; Italic Characters; Underline Characters**

Formatting charts—**Chart Formatting; Charts; Chart Text; Chart Types**

Formatting database forms—**Alignment; Coloring Database Forms; Field Lines; Field Names**

Formatting numbers and dates—**Alignment; Currency Symbols; Date Formats; Formatting Numbers; Fractions; Percentages; Scientific Notation; Time Formats**

Formatting pages—**Headers and Footers; Margins; Page Numbers; Page Orientation; Page Setup**

Formatting paragraphs—**Bulleted Lists; Indents and Alignment; Line Spacing; Paragraph Breaks**

Formatting reports—**Alignment; Borders; Changing Fonts; Column Width; Formatting Numbers; Headers and Footers; Margins; Page Numbers; Page Orientation; Page Setup; Row Height**

Formatting spreadsheets and tables—**Alignment; AutoFormatting; Column Width; Gridlines; Row Height**

Setting tab stops—**Tabs**

Formatting Numbers

You can format numbers and dates by selecting the **cells** you want to format and choosing the Format Number command.

Use the Format radio buttons to select a formatting category.

Works displays the options available for the selected format.

Works displays a sample that shows how your current selections in the Format and Options boxes might look.

Formatting when you enter data

Sometimes it's easier to format numbers and dates by entering the **value** in the format you want. For example, if you enter *$1,000.00* into a cell, the cell contains the value 1000, but Works automatically formats it to include a dollar sign, comma, and two decimal places.

Form Letter WorksWizard The Form Letter **WorksWizard** leads you through the process of creating a letter that you can mail to everyone in a **database**. It also helps you to limit the mailing to people who meet criteria you specify, and to sort the records before printing.

Mail Merge

Forms

A form is a screen representation of a paper data-entry form. (But when you add pictures, borders, and fancy fonts, it's more attractive than an ordinary paper form.) When you examine a **database** in **form view**, Works displays one **record** at a time.

Creating a Form

Works has several **WorksWizards** that can lead you through the process of creating a form, or you can follow these steps:

1 Choose the File Create New File command.

2 In the Startup dialog box, choose Database.

3 After an explanatory message (press Enter to clear it), Works displays a new, blank database form.

continues

Forms *(continued)*

4 To insert a **field**, position the **insertion point** where you want the field. Type the **field name** followed by a colon and then press Enter. Works displays the Field Size dialog box.

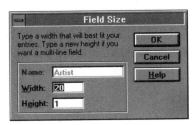

5 The Width and Height specify the size of the **field lines** on the form, but do not restrict the amount of data you can enter into a field. (You can change the size at any time; see **Resizing Fields**.) Press Enter to close the Field Size dialog box.

6 To insert text other than a field name, simply position the insertion point and type.

7 You can dress up your form by **adding pictures**, **changing fonts**, using **borders**, and so on.

Printing blank forms

Your Works form might look so good that you'll want printed copies to use for collecting data. Here's how: In form view, press Ctrl+End to display the blank form after the last record. Then choose the File Print command and select the Current Record Only radio button.

❖ **Entering Data; Shading**

Formula Bar

The formula bar is the area beneath the **toolbar**, and it's the place where you enter **values** and **formulas** into **cells** or **fields**.

The formula bar displays the contents of the **active cell**. If you click the formula or press F2, you can edit the cell's contents.

Formulas

In Works, you use a formula in a spreadsheet **cell** or database **field** when you want to calculate a **value**. A formula must begin with an equal sign (=), and it can contain values, **cell addresses**, cell **names, functions**, and the following arithmetic operators:

Operator	What it does	Example, result
^	Raises to a power	=5^2, 25
*	Multiplies	=5*2, 10
/	Divides	=5/2, 2.5
+	Adds	=5+2, 7
−	Subtracts	=5−2, 3
=	Returns TRUE if equal	=5=2, FALSE
<>	Returns TRUE if not equal	=5<>2, TRUE
<	Returns TRUE if less than	=5<2, FALSE
>	Returns TRUE if greater than	=5>2, TRUE
<=	Returns TRUE if less than or equal to	=5<=2, FALSE
>=	Returns TRUE if greater than or equal to	=5>=2, TRUE

The power of formulas, of course, is not determining that 5 is, in fact, greater than 2. More likely, you'll want to perform calculations based on the values in other cells. For example, the formula =C2−C18 subtracts the value in C18 from the value in cell C2.

continues

Formulas *(continued)*

Better looking formulas

You can make your formulas easier to read by naming cells before you
enter the formula. The previous example could then read =Price–Cost.

Form View

Form view is one of the two basic ways to view
information in a **database**. (The other is **list view**.) Form
view shows a single **record**. Press F9 to switch between
form view and list view.

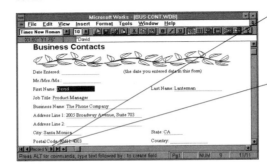

To view the
next record,
click here
or press
Ctrl+PgDn.

To skip to
the blank
record at
the end of
the
database,
click here
or press
Ctrl+End.

Field Lines; Views

Fractions

Normally, Works displays numbers as decimal values. But if you're tracking stock prices or maintaining an inventory that includes shoe sizes, you'll want to see fractions. To display numbers as fractions, select the cells you want and choose the Format Number command. Mark Fraction and, optionally, specify the denominator.

Entering a Fraction

To enter a fractional value, type a space between the integer and the fraction, like this: *4 1/2*.

Entering values less than 1

When you enter a fractional value that is less than 1, be sure to type 0 (zero) and a space before the fraction (for example, *0 3/8*). Otherwise, Works interprets your entry as a date.

Formatting Numbers; Selecting Cells

Functions

A function is a predefined **formula** that makes it much easier to perform complex calculations in a **spreadsheet** or **database**. To use a function, enter its name in a formula. After the name, type the input for the formula enclosed in parentheses. (Each input value is called an "**argument**," but let's not bicker.) If a function requires more than one argument, separate them with a comma. For example:

PMT(Principal,Rate/12,360)

Name

Arguments

continues

Functions *(continued)*

Calculations for investments, loans, and depreciation—**Financial Functions**

Conditional tests—**Logical Functions**

Functions for displaying and calculating dates and times—**Date and Time Functions**

Functions for displaying error values—**Informational Functions**

Functions for formatting, finding, and manipulating text strings—**Text Functions**

References to other cells—**Lookup and Reference Functions**

The stuff you never understood in high school—**Mathematical and Trigonometric Functions**

The stuff you never understood in college—**Statistical Functions**

If you always lose arguments

The name and syntax of some Works functions are not easy to remember, but Works can prompt you. In the spreadsheet module, choose the Insert Function command. The Insert Function dialog box lists all the available functions (you can shorten the list by marking a category) and shows the names of the arguments each function requires. Select a function and choose OK to insert it in the **formula bar**.

Go To You can jump directly to a specific place in the active document by choosing the Edit Go To command or using its keyboard shortcut, F5:

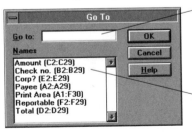

You can jump directly to a page (word processor), **cell** (spreadsheet), or **record** (database) by typing its number in the Go To text box.

The Names list box lists all the **bookmarks** (word processor), range **names** (spreadsheet), or **field names** (database) that you have defined; select one to go to it.

H

Gridlines  Gridlines are the dotted lines that delineate the **cells** in the spreadsheet or in the database **list view**. You can make them appear and disappear by choosing the View Gridlines command.

Printing gridlines

The View Gridlines command controls only the display of gridlines. To control whether gridlines print, choose the File Page Setup command, select the Other Options tab, and use the Print Gridlines check box.

Chart Formatting

Headers and Footers A header is text that appears at the top of every page; a footer appears at the bottom of every page. You can use headers and footers to print page numbers, titles, filenames, dates, and other information.

Creating a Header or Footer

1 Choose the View Headers And Footers command.

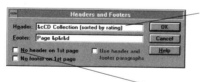

2 Type the text you want for the header and footer. You can include any of the codes shown on the next page.

3 Mark these check boxes if you want the header or footer to print on all pages except the first page.

continues

Headers and Footers *(continued)*

To do this	Insert this code
Left align characters that follow	&l
Right align characters that follow	&r
Center characters that follow	&c
Print the page number	&p
Print the filename	&f
Print the date	&d
Print the date in long format	&n
Print the time	&t
Print a single ampersand	&&

Creating a Multiline Header or Footer

In the word processor, headers and footers can contain multiple lines
and pictures, and you can use all the word processor's formatting
capabilities. To create such a header, mark the Use Header And Footer
Paragraphs check box in the Headers And Footers dialog box. Works
inserts two special paragraphs at the beginning of your document,
which are identified with a letter in the left margin. Format these
paragraphs directly instead of using the codes in the table above.

Header
Footer

Margins; Page Numbers

Help

You only need to remember one thing: F1. Press that key whenever you have a question, and Works displays help about the module or dialog box that you're currently using.

If you want continual nudges, choose the Help Cue Cards command, which opens a window with step-by-step instructions for most Works tasks.

Hiding Fields

In **list view**, you'll sometimes find it useful to hide one or more **fields** so you can view nonadjacent fields side by side. To do so, drag the **field name's** right border to the left until you can no longer see the field. Alternatively, you can select the field and then choose the Format Field Width command. Set the width to 0.

Restoring Hidden Fields

If you want to display a field in list view that you have hidden, follow these steps:

1 Choose the Edit Go To command.

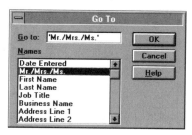

2 Select the name of the field you want to restore, and then choose OK.

3 Choose the Format Field Width command.

4 Enter a width greater than 0.

Hiding Records  You can hide **records** that you're not interested in viewing. Hidden records do not print, nor are they included in **reports**, form letters, **mailing labels**, or other **mail merge** operations.

Hiding Records

You can hide certain records in any of these ways:

- Choose the Edit Find command and mark All Records. Works hides the records that don't contain the search text you specify.

- Use a query. Works hides records that don't satisfy the query.

- Select one or more records and choose the View Hide Record command.

Viewing Hidden Records

You can make all the hidden records visible and make all the visible records hidden by choosing the View Switch Hidden Records command.

To make all records visible again, choose the View Show All Records command.

Finding Records; Queries

Hyphenation  Works can automatically hyphenate words in your document, which reduces the raggedness of the right margin. To do so, choose the Tools Hyphenation command.

Mark the Hyphenate CAPS check box if it's OK to hyphenate words that are all uppercase.

Mark the Confirm check box if you want Works to stop and show you each proposed hyphen, giving you an opportunity to change its position or prevent hyphenating a word.

The Hot Zone balances the number of hyphens vs. raggedness. A narrow hot zone hyphenates more words to make the margin less ragged; a wide hot zone results in fewer hyphens and a more ragged margin.

Optional hyphens and nonbreaking hyphens

An optional hyphen is one that the **word wrap** feature in Works uses only if it falls near the end of the line; otherwise it is invisible. The Tools Hyphenation command inserts optional hyphens where it deems necessary. You can also insert an optional hyphen by pressing Ctrl+hyphen.

Sometimes you'll want to be sure that a certain hyphen doesn't fall at the end of a line, such as the hyphen in a compound name. In this case, use a nonbreaking hyphen. Press Ctrl+Shift+hyphen.

Importing Files

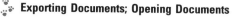

Exporting Documents; Opening Documents

Indents and Alignment  Indents are the space between the text and the page **margins**; alignment refers to the way text lines up with the margins. You control paragraph indents and alignment with the Format Paragraph command.

Use predefined indents and alignment

Select the Quick Formats tab to see a list of predefined paragraph formats—saving you the effort of specifying indents, alignment, and **line spacing**.

Informational Functions The four informational **functions** work with cells that contain the **value** ERR (for "error") or N/A ("not available"). For example, the following **formula** displays 1 (TRUE) if cell A5 contains N/A; otherwise it displays 0 (FALSE):

=ISNA(A5)

Naaah

To obtain the value N/A, you must use the NA() function. If you simply type *N/A* in the **formula bar**, Microsoft Works interprets it as text instead of a special value.

 Arguments

Inserting Columns and Rows 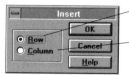 To insert a new column or row in a spreadsheet, choose the Insert Row/Column command.

Select Row to insert a row above the highlighted cell.

Select Column to insert a column to the left of the highlighted cell.

Inserting multiple columns or rows

To insert more than one column or row, select multiple cells before choosing the Insert Row/Column command. Works inserts one column or row for each selected column or row.

Adding Fields; Adding Records

Inserting Fields

Adding Fields; Mail Merge

Insertion Point The insertion point is the flashing vertical bar that shows where the characters you type will appear. You can move the insertion point by using the direction keys, or by clicking where you want it to be.

Italic Characters To change characters to *italic*, select the text (or the cells that contain the text) and then press Ctrl+I or click the Italic tool.

Labels

☆ **Chart Text; Mailing Labels**

Letterheads ◇ To create and use a custom letterhead, follow these steps:

1 Choose the File WorksWizards command. Select Letterhead and then press Enter. The **WorksWizard** guides you through the process of creating a letterhead.

2 Make any modifications you want to the letterhead document.

3 Choose the File Save As command and then choose the Template button.

4 Type a name for your **template** and press Enter.

5 To create a letter, choose the File Templates command, select Custom in the Choose A Template Group drop-down list box, and select your letterhead template in the Choose A Template list box.

Line Spacing ◇ To adjust the space between the lines in a **paragraph**, before the paragraph, or after the paragraph, select the paragraph and then choose the Format Paragraph command. Select the Breaks and Spacing tab.

Enter a number in each of the three Line Spacing text boxes. If you enter a number alone, Works interprets it as a number of lines. (There are six lines per inch.) You can also specify spacing in inches (in or "), centimeters (cm), picas (pi), **points** (pt), or millimeters (mm) by appending the unit abbreviation to the number.

Using Auto spacing

If you type "Auto" in the Between Lines text box, Works sets the line spacing to the height of the tallest character in each line.

Row Height

Lists

Bulleted Lists

List View

List view is one of the two basic ways to view information in a **database**. (The other is **form view**.) List view displays the information in a **spreadsheet**-like format, where each **record** occupies one **row** and each **column** represents a **field**.

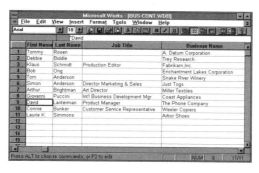

Gridlines; Views

Logical Functions

Works has six logical **functions**, which are based on the theory that everything—at least in the world of spreadsheets—is either true or false. In fact—except for the IF() function—the logical functions can return only one of two answers: 1 (TRUE) or 0 (FALSE). Logical functions are typically used to check for the presence (or absence) of certain conditions. The following example **formula** displays one message if the value of the range named Profit is greater than $10,000, and a different message if it is not:

=IF(Profit>10000,"Great news!","Uh-oh")

Displaying logical values as text

Normally, Works displays the result of a logical function as either 0 or 1. You can make your spreadsheet more legible by **formatting numbers** as True/False. Then cells that contain the value 0 display as FALSE; cells that contain any other numeric value display as TRUE.

Arguments; Comparing Values

Lookup and Reference Functions

The six lookup and reference **functions** can do things like tell you how many columns are in a range you specify or look up a **value** from a list or a range of **cells**. For example, this **formula** displays "Better" if the value of cell B5 is 2:

=CHOOSE(B5,"Good","Better","Best")

Arguments

Lotus 1-2-3

Lotus 1-2-3 is another **spreadsheet** program. Why mention it here? Because you can open and save Lotus 1-2-3 version 2.*x* worksheet files with Works. To do so, choose the File Open Existing File or File Save As command, and then select Lotus 1-2-3 in the List Files of Type list box.

Exporting Documents; Opening Documents; Saving Documents

Mailing Labels To create a mailing label, choose the Tools Envelopes And Labels command and select the Mailing Labels tab.

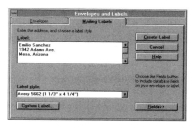

Printing a Single Label

1 Type the information you want on the label in the Label text box.

2 Select a label size from the Label Style drop-down list, or choose Custom Label to define a new size.

3 Choose Create Label, and Works inserts the label text at the beginning of your document.

4 To print the label, choose the File Print command and select the Mailing Labels radio button.

continues

Mailing Labels *(continued)*

Printing Labels from a Database

1 Open a word processor document.

2 Choose the Tools Envelopes And Labels command and select the Mailing Labels tab. Choose the Fields button.

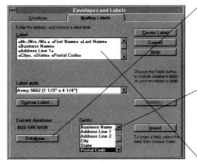

3 Choose Database to open the Choose Database dialog box. Select the database you want to use and press Enter.

4 Select each database field you want, and then choose Insert to insert a placeholder in the Label text box.

5a Insert spaces and punctuation as needed to separate the placeholders in the Label text box.

5b adjust layout, use return to create new line for each line of address.

6 Choose Create Label, and Works inserts the label text at the beginning of your document.

7 To print the labels, choose the File Print command and select the Mailing Labels radio button. Be sure the Print Merge check box is marked before you choose OK. (If you don't want to print a label for every record in the database, see **Hiding Records** or **Queries**.)

8 Works displays the Choose Database dialog box. Select the database whose records you want to print and choose OK.

Selecting Avery labels

The Label Style drop-down list shows lots of Avery labels. The 4000-series labels are for dot-matrix printers, and the 5000-series labels are for laser and inkjet printers. The other Avery products shown are metric sizes that are generally available only outside the United States.

Mail Merge  With the merge capabilities in Works, you can print a word processor document, such as a form letter or **envelope**, for every **record** in a **database**. Follow these steps:

1 If you haven't already, create a database. (See **Databases**.)

2 Create the word processor document. To include the contents of a **field** from the database, choose the Insert Database Field command. (The first time you choose Insert Database Field, the Current Database box shows None. Choose the Database button and then select a database from the list that appears.)

3 Select the field you want and choose Insert. Works inserts a placeholder in the document. Insert all the field placeholders you want; you can move and format them later. Choose Close when you're finished inserting field placeholders.

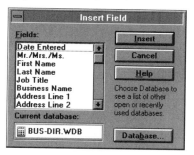

4 Format your document—including the field placeholders.

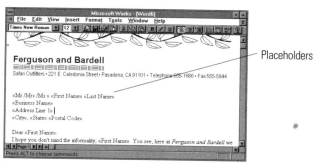

Placeholders

5 If you don't want to print a document for every record in a database, open the database and hide the records you don't want to include. You can hide records manually or with a **query**.

continues

Mail Merge *(continued)*

6 To print your documents (that's right, *documents*—one for each nonhidden record), switch to the word processor document and choose File Print. Be sure the Print Merge check box is marked before you choose OK.

7 Works displays the Choose Database dialog box. Select the database whose records you want to print and choose OK.

⁘ **Form Letter WorksWizard; Hiding Records; Mailing Labels**

Manual Calculation  Works normally recalculates all the **values** that change whenever you make an entry in a **cell**, which can slow you down if you have a very large spreadsheet. To tell Works to wait, choose the Tools Manual Calculation command. Then, when you want Works to calculate the spreadsheet, press F9.

Margins  Margins control the white space around the edge of a page. To set the margins, choose the File Page Setup command and select the Margins tab.

The Header Margin sets the distance between the top of the page and the top of the header. This entry must be smaller than the Top Margin, which specifies the distance from the top of the page to the top of the text.

The Footer Margin sets the distance from the bottom of the page to the top of the footer. This entry must be smaller than the Bottom Margin, the distance from the bottom of the page to the bottom of the text.

⁘ **Headers and Footers; Indents and Alignment**

M

Mathematical and Trigonometric Functions

Works has 17 **functions** that calculate logarithms, sines, square roots, and other fun things that can make complex mathematical **formulas**. Here's a sampling of what they can do:

Function	What it does
=INT(3.8)	Returns the integer portion of 3.8, which is 3
=LOG(100)	Returns the common logarithm of 100, which is 2
=SIN(1)	Returns the sine of 1, which is 0.841471
=PI()	Returns the value of π, which is 3.1415927

 Arguments

Microsoft Excel

Microsoft Excel is a **spreadsheet** program—the "big brother" of the spreadsheet and charting module in Works. It does everything Works does and then some. And then some more. But it's not my job to sell Excel; I mention it here because you might find it handy to use Works on your home or portable computer and Excel on your desktop computer. You'll see lots of similarities, and you can open and save your Excel version 4.0 and 5.0 worksheets in Works. You can also open Works spreadsheets in Excel.

Keep it simple

Did I mention that Excel has many more features and capabilities than Works? When you use Excel with a worksheet that you'll later open in Works, be sure you use only the features and **functions** supported by Works. If you insert one of Excel's convoluted functions, for example, Works changes it to 0 (zero) when you open the spreadsheet in Works.

 Exporting Documents; Opening Documents; Saving Documents

Microsoft Word

Microsoft Word is a word processor that does things you never imagined a word processor could do. And it coexists nicely with Works: Many of the menus, toolbar buttons, dialog boxes, and procedures are nearly the same, so it's easy to move back and forth between the programs. And your word processor documents can move back and forth easily too; you can open and save Word for Windows version 2.0 and 6.0 documents in Works.

Exporting Documents; Opening Documents; Saving Documents

Mixed Cell References

A mixed reference combines an **absolute cell reference** and a **relative cell reference**, allowing you to refer to cells so that only the **column** or only the **row** reference is absolute. Place a dollar sign ($) before the part of the reference that you want to maintain absolute. For example, B$6 contains a relative column reference (B) and an absolute row reference ($6).

If you copy a **cell** that contains such a reference, the absolute row or column reference remains unchanged, and the relative reference adjusts.

Modem Setup

Choose the Settings Modem command if you're not sure which communications port your modem is connected to. Then choose the Test button, and Works will figure out where your modem is attached.

The Advanced button is for the adventuresome. It displays a dialog box that lets you specify the codes that your modem understands. Fortunately for us squeamish types, the standard settings work with most modems.

❖ **Communication Settings; Options**

Moving Data

You can move data within a **database** or spreadsheet the same way you move text in a word processor document: You **drag-and-drop**, or use Edit Cut and Edit Paste.

❖ **Copying Data**

Moving Objects and Pictures

You can move objects (such as **Note-It** notes, **tables**, and **charts**) and pictures within a document by selecting the object and dragging it where you want it.

Alternatively, you can use the Edit Cut and Edit Paste commands.

❖ **Copying Objects and Pictures; Drag-and-Drop; Selecting Objects**

Moving Text

The easiest way to move selected text is to drag it to the desired location.

You can also move text by following these steps:

1 Select the text you want to move.

2 Choose the Edit Cut command, which removes the text from the document and places it on the **Clipboard**.

3 Place the **insertion point** where you want the text.

4 Choose the Edit Paste command.

❖ **Drag-and-Drop; Copying Text; Selecting Text**

Names

You can name a **cell** or a **range** of cells and then use that name in **formulas** and dialog boxes instead of using a **cell address**. To name a cell or a range, follow these steps:

1 Select the cell or range of cells.

2 Choose the Insert Range Name command. Works displays the Range Name dialog box.

3 Type the name in the Name text box. Range names can be up to 15 characters long. Existing range names appear in the Names list box.

Use labels as range names

If the topmost or leftmost cell in the highlighted range contains a label (in other words, text), Works proposes that text as the range name when you choose the Insert Range Name command.

❖ **Field Names; Filenames**

New Documents

To create a new document, choose the—what else?—File Create New File command.

Choose which type of document you want to create in the Create A New box.

❖ **Opening Documents**

Nonbreaking Spaces A nonbreaking space ensures that two words stay together on the same line. To insert a nonbreaking space, press Ctrl+Shift+Spacebar or choose the Insert Special Character command.

Special Characters

Nonprinting Characters Some **special characters** determine the appearance of a document by controlling, for example, where lines end and how words are hyphenated. Normally, these nonprinting characters do not appear on the screen, but you can see them by choosing the View All Characters command.

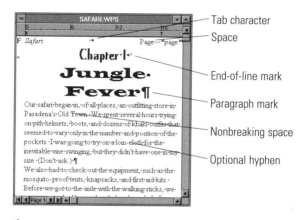

Tab character
Space
End-of-line mark
Paragraph mark
Nonbreaking space
Optional hyphen

Ending Lines; Hyphenation; Nonbreaking Spaces; Paragraphs

Note-It

Note-It is an accessory application that lets you put pop-up notes—identified by a cute icon of your choosing—in your word processor documents and database **forms**.

Creating a Note-It Note

Place the **insertion point** in the word processor document or database form where you want the note picture to appear, and then choose the Insert Note-It command.

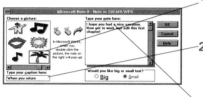

1 Select the picture that you want to mark your note.

2 Type the caption that you want to appear beneath the note picture.

3 Type the text that you want to pop up when you open the note.

Reading a Note-It Note

Simply double-click the note picture, and your note text pops up in a separate window. To close the note window, click anywhere or press any key.

⁙ **Deleting Objects; Moving Objects and Pictures; Object Linking and Embedding; Resizing Objects and Pictures**

0

Object Linking and Embedding

Object linking and embedding, commonly abbreviated as OLE (as in ¡Olé!), is a feature of Microsoft Windows. OLE lets you create a "compound document"—one that combines two or more types of documents. You use this feature (perhaps unknowingly) to place a table, **Note-It** note, or **ClipArt Gallery** picture in a word processor document, for example.

Creating a Compound Document

You'll never see "OLE" or "object linking and embedding" on a Works menu. Instead, you use the Insert menu, which has commands for most of the commonly used objects. The Insert Object command is a catchall that lets you insert any type of object that's available on your system. (*Object* is the technical term for the thing-from-another-application-that-you-want-to-place-in-a-document.)

Working with Objects

If you click an object in a Works document, a rectangular frame surrounds the object, and you can then copy, move, delete, or resize the object. If you double-click the object, the application that created the object takes over. With most object types, that means the application's menus and toolbar appear, and you can edit the object—all from within Works. When you're finished editing, just click outside the object, and the standard Works menu returns.

Creating objects—**Drag-and-Drop; Embedding and Linking Existing Objects; Embedding New Objects; Sharing Works Data**

Modifying objects—**Deleting Objects; Moving Objects and Pictures; Resizing Objects and Pictures**

Opening Documents To open a previously saved Works document, follow these steps:

1 Open the File menu. If the document you want to open is among the last four you used, its name appears at the bottom of the File menu and you can reopen it simply by choosing its name from this menu.

2 If the document isn't listed, choose the Open Existing File command.

3 Use the List Files of Type list box if you want to open a file that was saved in a format other than the Works format.

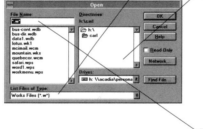

4 Use the Drives and Directories list boxes to specify where the document was saved. (Choose the Network button if the file is located on a network drive that you're not currently connected to.)

5 Select the filename in the File Name list box or type it in the File Name text box.

Protecting your original document

Sometimes you'll want to be sure that you don't inadvertantly change a previously saved document. You can protect a document by marking the Read Only check box in the Open dialog box. Works won't prevent you from making changes to the document while it's open, but you won't be able to resave it using the same name. You'll either have to abandon your changes or save the file under a new name—keeping the original file intact.

 File Organizer WorksWizard; New Documents

Options 🖐 🖥 🖨 🖨 The Options dialog box lets you make default settings for a handful of unrelated options—most of which you'll never need to change. To see what you can change, choose the Tools Options command.

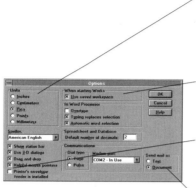

The Units section determines the units of measure that appear on the **ruler**, in **formatting** and **Page Setup** dialog boxes, and so on.

Mark this box if you want to automatically restore the saved **workspace** when you start Works.

If your printer has an envelope feeder, mark this box before you print **envelopes**.

If you use electronic mail to send Works documents to others, mark Document if the recipient also has Works; otherwise mark Text.

Who wouldn't want "helpful mouse pointers"?

If you use a portable computer with an LCD display, you might prefer to clear Use 3-D Dialogs and Helpful Mouse Pointers. And you can gain some screen space by clearing Show Status Bar.

Page Breaks

A page break determines where a new page begins when you print a document. Works figures out the location of page breaks automatically—but you can override its actions.

Page Breaks in Word Processor Documents

Automatic page breaks are indicated by a » symbol in the left margin.

To insert a manual page break, press Ctrl+Enter. A dotted line across the window indicates a manual page break, which you can delete or move like any other character.

You can restrict automatic page breaks so that certain paragraphs are not separated by a page break. See **Paragraph Breaks**.

Page Breaks in Spreadsheets, Database List View, and Reports

To insert a manual page break in a spreadsheet or a database's **list view** or **report view**, select the **row** (**record**) below or the **column** (**field**) to the right of where you want to insert a page break. Then choose Insert Page Break. Works indicates a manual page break with a dashed line.

To delete a manual page break, select the row below or the column to the right of the page break. Then choose the Insert Delete Page Break command.

Page Breaks in Database Form View

To insert a manual page break in a database **form**, place the **insertion point** where you want the page break and choose Insert Page Break. Works indicates the page break with a dotted line across the window.

Normally Works prints each database form on a new page. If you prefer to save a tree and print as many forms as will fit on each sheet, choose the File Page Setup command and select the Other Options tab. Then clear the Page Breaks Between Records check box.

Finding Text; Special Characters

P

Page Numbers You can number the pages of any document you print by including the &p code in the header or footer.

In a word processor document, you can insert a page number anywhere. To do so, choose the Insert Special Character command and then select the Print Page Number radio button.

Setting the beginning page number

If you want to start numbering pages with a number other than 1, choose File Page Setup and select the Other Options tab. Then type the number you want in the 1st Page Number box.

 Headers and Footers

Page Orientation You can print your pages in either portrait (vertical) or landscape (horizontal) orientation. To select the orientation, choose the File Page Setup command and select the Source, Size And Orientation tab.

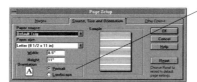

Select the
orientation
you want.

P

Page Setup 🖎 📇 📇   Choose the File Page Setup command
to display the Page Setup dialog box, which lets you set
margins, **header and footer** locations, paper size, **page
orientation**, beginning **page number**, and sundry print-
related options for each Works module.

> **Endnotes; Field Lines; Footnotes; Gridlines; Page Breaks;
> Reports**

Page Tab 🖎 📇 📇 📇   Some dialog boxes contain way too
many options to be crammed into such a tiny space.
Microsoft's solution? Page tabs along the top of the dialog
box, which divide the dialog box into groups of related
options. You can see such tabs in the Page Setup dialog
box, among others. To see the options under each tab,
click the tab or hold the Alt key and press the tab's under-
lined letter.

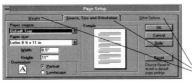

Page tabs

Pagination 🖎 📇 📇   Microsoft Works automatically figures
out where each printed page in a document should begin.
You can override its choices by putting in your own **page
breaks** or by restricting **paragraph breaks**.

P

Paragraph Breaks

You can prevent Works from splitting a paragraph over a page boundary, and you can ensure that two paragraphs are not separated by a page boundary. To do so, select the paragraphs you want to control, choose Format Paragraph, and select the Breaks And Spacing tab.

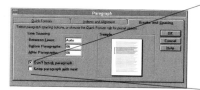

Mark the Don't Break Paragraph check box to prevent Works from placing an automatic **page break** within the selected paragraphs.

Mark the Keep Paragraph With Next check box to prevent Works from placing an automatic page break between the selected paragraphs and the paragraph that follows. (Headings, for example, benefit from this setting, because they look really dumb when they are at the bottom of a page.)

Paragraphs

A paragraph (at least as Works views it) is some text—words, sentences, whatever—that ends with a paragraph mark. You insert a paragraph mark by pressing Enter. (Choose View All Characters to see the paragraph marks, which look like this: ¶.)

It's important to think of paragraphs in the same way that Works does, because **formatting** and **pagination** are based on paragraphs.

Indents and Alignment; Line Spacing; Paragraph Breaks

P

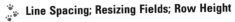

Paragraph Spacing

:·: **Line Spacing; Resizing Fields; Row Height**

Pasting

You can copy the contents of the Clipboard to the active window by choosing Edit Paste, pressing Ctrl+V, or clicking the Paste tool. The **Clipboard** contents are inserted at the **insertion point** or in the **active cell**. If you have selected text, the Clipboard contents replace the selection.

For additional paste options, choose Edit Paste Special. The dialog box that appears varies depending on the contents of the Clipboard and the module you are pasting into, but as you select the different options, an explanation in the dialog box spells out what'll happen if you choose OK.

:·: **Object Linking and Embedding**

Patterns

You can apply predefined patterns, such as parallel lines or tiny dots, to the background of database **fields**, **field names**, and labels; the background of spreadsheet **cells**; and **chart** components. You make a pattern choice when you select a color for those elements.

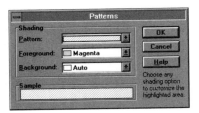

:·: **Shading**

P

Percentages

Percentages are decimal **values**, such as 0.15, that are formatted like this: 15%. To enter a percentage in a **cell**, you can enter its decimal value and then format it. Or you can simply type it as a percentage, including the percent sign (%).

⁙ **Formatting Numbers**

Phone Settings

Before you can connect to another computer, you need to tell Works how to make the connection. You do so by choosing the Settings Phone command.

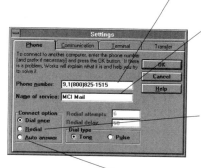

Type the phone number, including any codes you need to get an outside line. A comma tells the modem to pause for a second or two.

Your entry in the Name Of Service text box is added to the bottom of the Phone menu, so you can easily reconnect later.

Select the Redial radio button if you want Works to retry if it can't connect the first time—such as when it gets a busy signal.

If you want your modem to answer incoming calls, select Auto Answer. Works then ignores all other settings in the Phone Settings dialog box.

⁙ **Communication Settings; Protocol; Terminal Settings**

Points

A point is a unit of measure used by printers and typographers to specify the size of type. A point is about 1/72 of an inch. The type size shown on the **toolbar** and in the Font And Style dialog box is expressed in points. You can also use points to specify other measurements, such as the size of **margins**. To do so, append the abbreviation pt to the numeric measurement.

❖ **Changing Fonts**

Positioning Fields

In a database **form**, you can move a **field** and its **field name**. Click the field to select it, and then drag it to its new location.

Line up, everybody

Forms look better when the fields are aligned with each other. To facilitate alignment, be sure the Format Snap To Grid command is checked. (Choose it if it isn't checked.) This creates an invisible 12-lines-per-inch grid that form elements automatically align to when you move or resize them.

❖ **Drag-and-Drop; Protecting Form Designs**

Precedents

Precedents are **cells** that supply **values** to the **formulas** in other cells. If cell A1 contains the formula =B1+C1, then cells B1 and C1 are precedents. They must provide values before the formula in cell A1 can calculate.

Calculation order

When you rely on precedents to provide values, be aware of the order in which a spreadsheet calculates. If a precedent is below or to the right of a **dependent** cell, you might get incorrect results. When Microsoft Works calculates a spreadsheet, it calculates each cell in the first **column** from top to bottom, then calculates each cell in the second column from top to bottom, and so on.

❖ **Dependents; ERR Message**

Printing

 To print the **document** in the active **document window**, choose the File Print command. (If you've already made the appropriate settings in the Print dialog box, you can bypass it by clicking the Print tool.) But I'm getting ahead of myself.

Before You Print

1 Create a document and format it as desired.

2 Use the **Page Setup** dialog box to select a paper size, set **margins**, and so on.

3 Choose the File Printer Setup command to select a printer if you have more than one connected to your system.

4 Choose File **Print Preview** to see how your printed pages will look.

When You're Ready to Print

Choose the File Print command to display the Print dialog box.

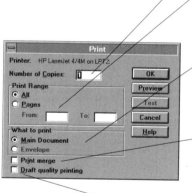

Type the number of document copies you want.

If you don't want to print the whole document, select Pages and type the numbers of the first and last pages you want to print.

The What To Print section appears only when you print a word processor document that contains an envelope or mailing label.

Mark the Print Merge check box if you want to replace a word processor document's field placeholders with the contents of database fields.

Marking Draft Quality Printing prevents charts, database forms, graphics, and different fonts from printing, which can speed up printing.

continues

117

Printing *(continued)*

If you don't want to print a complete document

Whenever you print a multipage document, you can specify a range of pages to print. But there are other ways to print part of a spreadsheet or database:

- To print only part of a spreadsheet, select the range of cells you want to print and then choose the Format Set Print Area command. (To reset the print area so the whole spreadsheet prints, choose Insert Range Name, select Print Area, choose the Delete button, and then choose OK.)

- To print certain records from a database, see **Hiding Records** to find out how to hide records you don't want to print. You can also print a single record in form view: Display the record and then select the Current Record Only radio button in the Print dialog box.

 Envelopes; Mailing Labels; Mail Merge

Print Preview

Save a tree and a trip to the printer by previewing your documents on screen before you print them. Choose the File Print Preview command.

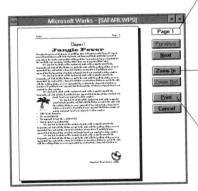

Works displays the page number of the currently displayed page. Choose Previous or Next to flip through the pages.

Works starts the preview by displaying a full page. Choose Zoom In for a closer look.

If everything looks OK, choose Print. If you need to make corrections first, choose Cancel—and pat yourself on the back for saving paper.

Protecting Cells and Fields

You can prevent changes to spreadsheet **cells** or database **fields** by protecting them. You can protect certain cells—ones that contain complex **formulas** or data that you don't want to change—and leave other parts of the document unprotected so you can enter new data. Protecting cells and fields is a two-step process:

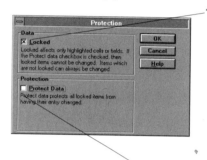

1 Lock the cells you want protected; unlock the cells you want to be able to change. You do this by selecting the cells you want to lock or unlock. Then choose the Format Protection command. Mark the Locked check box to lock (protect), or clear it to unlock the highlighted cells. Then choose OK.

2 To enable the cell locking you have set, you must turn on protection. To do so, choose Format Protection and mark the Protect Data check box. Choose OK.

Removing protection

When a document is protected, Works prevents you from changing the contents of locked cells or fields. And it also disables many other commands that control **formatting**, add or delete rows or columns, and so on. To restore these capabilities, you must turn off protection. Choose Format Protection, clear the Protect Data check box, and choose OK.

Protecting Form Designs

P

Protecting Form Designs

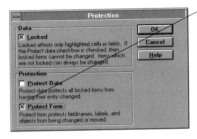 After you design a beautiful database **form** and have positioned all the **fields**, labels, and pictures where you want them, you don't want anyone to muck around with it. Fear not. While in **form view**, choose the Format Protection command.

Mark the Protect Form check box to prevent changes to **field names**, field locations, field sizes, **fonts**, **colors**, **shading**, objects, and labels.

Protecting a form does not protect the data in the database, so you can continue to enter and edit data while the form is protected.

Form protection affects list view too

When you use **list view** to examine a form-protected database, you'll find that you can't add or delete fields, nor can you change field names. To restore this capability, you must switch to form view, choose Format Protection, and clear the Protect Form check box.

Protecting Cells and Fields

Protocol

In Microsoft Works, protocol has nothing to do with the way you address the queen of England—unless you're sending files to her via modem. The error-checking method two modem-connected computers use to exchange files is called a protocol, and both computers must use the same protocol. Works supports four popular protocols: Zmodem, Ymodem, Xmodem, and Kermit. To select a protocol, follow these steps:

1 Choose the Settings Transfer command.
2 Select a protocol in the Transfer Protocol list box.
3 Choose OK.

Which protocol to use?

Your choice is limited to the protocols supported by the computer you're communicating with. The list of protocols above shows them in order of desirability (i.e., speed, reliability, and features), so if the other computer supports more than one of the Works-supported protocols, select the best one supported by both computers.

 Sending and Receiving Files; Sending and Receiving Text

Queries

A query searches your **database** to find **records** that meet criteria you specify. You might, for example, want to list all your customers who live in California and who don't smoke. When you apply a query, Microsoft Works hides the records that don't match your query criteria, leaving the records that *do* match visible in **list view** and **form view**. (And when you create **reports** or use **mail merge** to print **envelopes** or **mailing labels**, Works includes only the visible records—so a query is a good way to select the records to include in those operations.)

continues

Q

Queries *(continued)*

Creating a Query

1 Choose the Tools Create New Query command.

2 Type a name for your query (15 characters or less) if you're not satisfied with "Query1."

3 In the first Choose A Field To Compare drop-down list box, select the **field** you want to use for the first criterion.

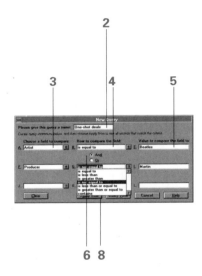

4 Select an option from the How To Compare The Field drop-down list.

5 In the Value To Compare The Field To text box, type the text that you want to compare.

6 If you want to add another criterion, select the And or Or radio button. If you select And, a record satisfies the query only if *both* criteria are true. If you select Or, a record satisfies the query if *either* criterion is true.

7 Repeat steps 3 through 6 to add a second and third criterion if you want.

8 Choose the Apply Now button, and Works displays a list of the records that match your query.

Q

Wildcards

You can use wildcards in the Value To Compare The Field To box to widen the scope of your query. Works recognizes two wildcards: A question mark (?) represents any single character, and an asterisk (*) represents any number of characters. To find either "Beatles" or "Beetles," for example, type *Be?tles*. Or to find everyone who lives on Colorado Street, type *Colorado St*.

Reusing a Query

Works saves up to eight queries with a database document. To reuse a query you've previously created, choose the View Apply Query command, select the query name, and choose OK. (This command isn't available in **query view**; you must first switch to list view or form view.)

Deleting a Query

If you want to create a new query when the database already has eight queries, you must delete one. To do so, choose the Tools Delete Query command, select a query name, and choose Delete. Choose OK when you're finished deleting queries.

 Finding Records; Hiding Records

Query View Query view looks much like **form view**, but instead of displaying **field** contents, each field can contain a query sentence.

You create the simplest query sentences by typing the same text you would type in the New Query dialog box's Value To Compare The Field To box—except you type it in the field.

But query view lets you create the most complex **queries**. In addition to the basic comparisons you can make with a simple query, query sentences can include mathematical **formulas** and **functions**. And unlike simple queries, you're not limited to just three criteria.

continues

Query View *(continued)*

Here are some example query sentences:

To find records where	Use this query sentence
Cost is greater than $1 and less than $10	>1#AND#<10
Last contact was in the past 10 days	>NOW()−10
Total value is greater than $1000	=(Cost*Quantity)>1000

After you create a query in query view, switch to **list view** or **form view** to see the results.

Use simple queries to learn query syntax

To see an example of a query sentence, create a simple query (see **Queries**), and then choose the Query View button.

∴ **Finding Records; Hiding Records; Views**

Range   A range is a group of adjacent **cells** or database **fields**. You'll often find it necessary to refer to a range in **formulas**. To refer to a range, you specify the **cell addresses** of the upper left and lower right corners of the range, separated by a colon.

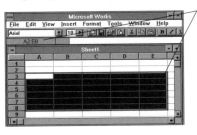

As indicated to the left of the **formula bar**, the address of the selected range is A3:E8.

∴ **Absolute Cell References; Mixed Cell References; Names; Relative Cell References**

Records

A record contains the data for a single "thing" (whatever "things" your database tracks, such as customers, compact discs, or store inventory). Each record is divided into **fields**. In **form view**, a single record is displayed. In **list view**, each record occupies one row.

A Microsoft Works database can contain up to 32,000 records.

 Adding Records; Deleting Records; Hiding Records; Scrolling; Sorting Records

Redo

If you change a document and then change your mind, choose the Edit Undo command. But if you change your mind again, choose the Edit Redo command, and your change is redone. You can continue this cycle endlessly if you like, but you'll probably tire of it quickly.

Undo

Relative Cell References

A relative cell reference is a **cell address** that Works adjusts if it's part of a **formula** that you copy. By default, all cell references are relative unless you add dollar signs to make them absolute. Maybe this example will help:

	A	B
1	5	
2	7	
3		2
4		

Cell A2 contains the formula =A1+2. A1 is a relative reference.

If you copy the formula from cell A2 to cell B3, Works adjusts the formula in cell B3 to read =B2+2. When you copy the formula to the right one column and down one row, Works changes the address so that it still refers to the cell immediately above the formula cell.

 Absolute Cell References; Mixed Cell References

Replacing Cell or Field Contents 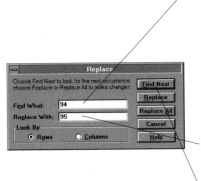 The Edit Replace command searches for **cells** or **fields** that contain the text, numbers, or formula that you specify and then replaces it. To use the Edit Replace command, follow these steps:

1 Select the **range** of cells or fields you want Works to search.

2 Choose the Edit Replace command.

3 In the Find What text box, type the characters you want to find. You can enter text, numbers, a **formula**, or part of a formula. Note that Works searches only the formulas in cells or fields—not the **values** produced by the formulas.

4 Type your replacement text in the Replace With text box.

5 Choose Find Next. Works searches until it finds your text and then pauses.

6 Choose Replace to replace the found occurrence or choose Find Next to continue searching without replacing. If you're sure of yourself, choose Replace All to find and replace all occurrences within the selected range.

Editing Cells; Editing Records; Finding Cells; Finding Records

R

Replacing Text ✍ Choose the Edit Replace command to find text you specify and then—at your option—replace it with other text. To use the Edit Replace command, follow these steps:

1 Select the text you want to search. If you want to search the entire document, don't select any text.

2 Choose the Edit Replace command.

3 In the Find What text box, type the text you want to find.

4 Type your replacement text in the Replace With text box.

3   4

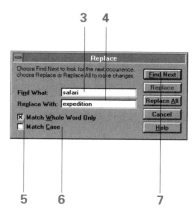

5   6   7

5 If you want Works to find only whole-word occurrences of the text, mark the Match Whole Word Only check box.

6 If you want Works to find only text that matches exactly, including capitalization, mark the Match Case check box.

7 Choose Find Next. Works searches until it finds your text and then pauses.

8 Choose Replace to replace the found occurrence or choose Find Next to continue searching without replacing. If you're sure of yourself, choose Replace All to find and replace all occurrences within the selected range.

⁘ **Editing Text; Finding Text**

127

Reports Reports provide a way to view and analyze your **database** in ways not possible with **form view** and **list view**. With a report, you can:

- Specify which fields to include and where to place them on the page—without modifying the database or its **form**

- Sort and group records based on field contents

- Perform calculations on fields and groups of records to provide summary information

- Add titles, headings, and other text to embellish the report

A report includes only records that are not hidden. You can use a **query** to hide the records you're not interested in before you print a report.

Creating a Report

1 Choose the Tools Create New Report command. Works displays the New Report dialog box.

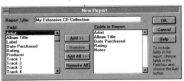

2 In the Report Title box, type a title for your report. The title appears at the top of the first page.

3 Select each field you want to include in the report and choose the Add >> button.

4 Choose OK. Works displays the Report Statistics dialog box.

5 For each field in the report, you can mark one or more calculations. Works places the results of the calculations at the end of the report.

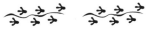

Works uses **report view** to display the report definition. You can modify the report by **adding rows and columns**, **formatting**, entering text and **formulas**, and so on. To see the results of your report, choose the File **Print Preview** command. To print your report, choose File Print.

Sorting and Grouping Records

By default, a report displays nonhidden records in the same order they appear in **list view** or **form view**, but you can change that. To do so, follow these steps while the report definition is displayed:

1 Choose the Tools Sort Records command.

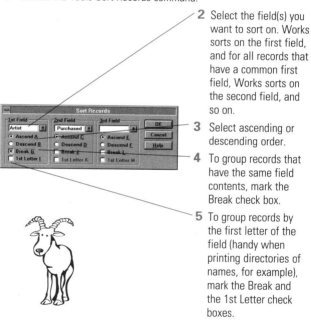

2 Select the field(s) you want to sort on. Works sorts on the first field, and for all records that have a common first field, Works sorts on the second field, and so on.

3 Select ascending or descending order.

4 To group records that have the same field contents, mark the Break check box.

5 To group records by the first letter of the field (handy when printing directories of names, for example), mark the Break and the 1st Letter check boxes.

Reusing a Report

Works saves up to eight reports with a database document. (It automatically saves a report when you create it.) To reuse a report you've previously created, choose the View Report command, select the report name, and choose OK.

continues

Reports *(continued)*

Deleting a Report

If you want to create a new report when the database already has eight reports, you must delete one. To do so, choose the Tools Delete Report command, select a report name, and choose Delete. Choose OK when you're finished deleting reports.

∴ **Hiding Records; Page Setup; Printing**

Report View

Report view shows your **report** definition. In report **view**, you can modify your report: add or delete columns or rows; add text, fields, or **formulas**; and format the output by adjusting **column width** or **row height**, **changing fonts**, and so on.

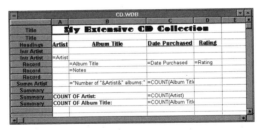

Report Rows

A report definition uses several different types of rows; the type is identified at the left end of the row. When you use Insert Row/Column to add a new row, Works asks which type of row you want to insert.

Type	What it does
Title	Prints at the top of the first page
Headings	Prints below the title on the first page, and at the top of all other pages
Intr *fieldname*	Appears at the beginning of each group if you sort and group records
Record	Prints fields from each record
Summ *fieldname*	Appears at the end of each group if you sort and group records
Summary	Prints at the end of the report

Resizing Fields  Microsoft Works asks you to specify a field size when you add a new field, but you're not stuck with it forever.

You must set sizes in **form view** and **list view** independently. Resizing a field in one view has no effect on the other.

Resizing a Field in Form View

1 Be sure that the form is not protected. Choose the Format Protection command, clear the Protect Form check box, and choose OK.

2 Select the field you want to resize.

3 Drag one of the resizing handles.

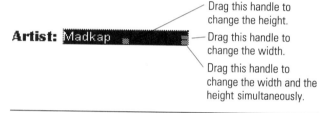

Drag this handle to change the height.

Drag this handle to change the width.

Drag this handle to change the width and the height simultaneously.

Resizing a Field in List View

To adjust the width, move the mouse pointer to the border at the right side of the **field name** at the top of the column. Then drag the border to the desired width.

To adjust the height, drag the border below the record number at the left end of the row.

Do mice scare you?

Instead of dragging, you can choose the Format Field Size command (form view) or the Format Field Width and Format Record Height commands (list view). Using the commands allows more precise sizing, and in list view the commands allow you to adjust multiple fields or records. Select the fields or records you want to resize before you choose a command.

continues

Resizing Fields *(continued)*

Making it fit

You can quickly adjust the width of a field in list view so that it perfectly contains the record with the longest field contents. Simply double-click the field name at the top of the column you want to adjust.

❖ **Column Width; Protecting Form Designs; Row Height**

Resizing Objects and Pictures 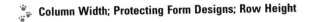 To change the
size of an object or picture, click the object to select it. Then drag the sizing handles—the little gray squares along the object's borders.

Maintaining proportions

Drag one of the corner handles to change an object's size without distorting it.

❖ **Object Linking and Embedding; Protecting Form Designs**

Resizing Windows ❖ To resize the Microsoft
Works **application window** or one of its **document windows**, use the mouse to drag its border until it's the size you want.

Tidying up your workspace

Your **workspace** can get cluttered if you open several **documents**. You needn't close them to restore order. Minimize the ones you want "on the back burner" by clicking the downward-pointing arrow in the document window's title bar. Then choose the Window Cascade or Window Tile command to neatly arrange the remaining open document windows.

❖ **Control-Menu Commands**

Row Height

 You can change the height of a row with the mouse or with the Format Row Height command.

Drag the border below the row number to change the height of that row.

The perfect row height

To adjust the row height to fit the tallest characters in the row, double-click the row number or mark the Best Fit check box in the Row Height dialog box.

Rows

In **list view**, every database **record** occupies a row. You can apply anything you know about spreadsheet rows (such as how to adjust the **row height** or select rows) to records.

 Inserting Columns and Rows; Selecting Columns and Rows

Ruler

The ruler, which appears at the top of each word processor **document window**, shows indents and tab settings. But the ruler is more than a pretty thing to look at: You can click the ruler to set a tab stop, or drag the indent and tab-stop markers to change the settings for the selected paragraphs.

To display the ruler if it isn't there—or to hide it if it's in your way—choose the View Ruler command.

First-line indent

Right margin

Default tab stops (Tab stops you set are shown as arrows.)

Left indent

 Indents and Alignment; Options; Tabs

S

Saving Documents To save the document

that's displayed in the active document window, click the Save tool, press Ctrl+S, or choose the File Save command.

Saving a Document You've Already Saved

If the document has been saved before, Works promptly replaces the old version with the latest version.

Saving a Document for the First Time

If you're working on a new document, Works displays the Save As dialog box.

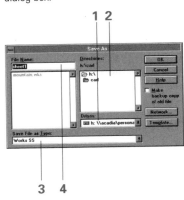

1 2

3 4

1 Select the disk drive where you want to save the file.

2 Select a directory.

3 If you want to save the file in a format that can be read by another program, select that program in the Save File As Type drop-down list box.

4 Type a **filename** of eight characters or less. (Works automatically appends the appropriate extension.)

Changing a document's name

To change the name of a document that you've already saved, choose the File Save As command instead of File Save. Works then presents the Save As dialog box shown above, and you can type a new filename.

.: Exporting Documents

Saving the Workspace

You can save the name, window size, and window position of all open documents (including those that have been minimized to an icon) by choosing File Save Workspace. Then whenever you start Works, it automatically opens those documents and restores the window layout exactly as it was when you last saved the workspace.

When you don't want those documents any more

To change the saved workspace, simply rearrange it to fit your new needs and choose File Save Workspace again. But if you don't want to use the saved workspace feature at all, choose Tools Options and clear the Use Saved Workspace check box.

❖ **Document Windows; Options**

Scientific Notation

When a cell with the general format contains a value that is too big or too small to fit in the cell's width, Microsoft Works uses **scientific notation**. In the illustration below, the **values** in column A are the same as those in column B; only the **column width** is different.

	A	B
1	250000000	2.5E+08
2	0.0000001	1E-07
3		

When it doesn't fit in the cell, Works displays the value 250,000,000 as 2.5E+08, which is equivalent to 2.5×10^8.

The value 0.0000001 is too small to fit neatly in this cell, so Works displays it as 1E–07, which is equivalent to 1×10^{-7}.

continues

Scientific Notation *(continued)*

If you wear a white lab coat

You might prefer to enter and view numbers in scientific notation. To enter a number in scientific notation, you can use either an uppercase or lowercase letter E, and you can omit the plus sign if the exponent is positive.

To be sure that numbers are displayed in scientific notation, choose Format Number and select Exponential. You can also specify the number of significant digits to display.

⁖ Formatting Numbers

Scripts

A script details the steps Works should take to perform a repetitive communications task, such as logging onto a service or downloading your new mail. Works can record your actions and save them as a script, and you can then modify the recorded script if you like.

Recording a Script

1 Choose the Tools Record Script command.

2 Select the Sign-on radio button to record a script that connects you to the other computer. Or select Other and type a name (15 characters or less) to record any other actions. Then choose OK.

3 Perform all the steps necessary to complete the task.

4 Choose the Tools End Recording command.

Playing Back a Script

To play back your script, you simply choose its name from the Tools menu.

Modifying a Script

1 Choose the Tools Edit Script command.

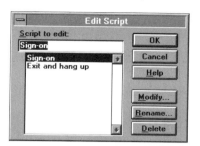

2 Select the name of the script you want to edit and then choose the Modify button.

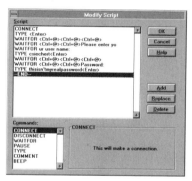

3 In the Script list box, select a command line you want to edit. Works displays an explanation of the command in the lower right corner.

You can edit or delete existing lines, or add new lines to your script.

Scrolling Like most other Windows-based applications, Works displays vertical and horizontal scroll bars that let you move around within a document when the entire document doesn't fit within its window.

Click a vertical scroll arrow to move up or down by one line or row.

Click the scroll bar above the scroll box to move up one screenful, or below the scroll box to move down one screenful.

Drag the scroll box to move through the document; the box's position in the bar indicates your relative position in the document.

The horizontal scroll bar provides similar controls for moving horizontally.

The **document window** for a word processor document or database **form** includes another set of controls in its lower left corner.

Click to move to the beginning of the document (the first page or record).

Click to move to the previous page or record.

Click to move to the next page or record.

Click to move to the end of the document.

Go To; Window Panes

Selecting

Practically anything you do in Microsoft Works—copying, moving, editing, formatting—affects the *selection*, which is typically highlighted by changing its displayed colors to white text on a black background.

Selecting cells in a spreadsheet or database list view—**Selecting Cells; Selecting Columns and Rows**

Selecting text—**Selecting Text**

Selecting embedded charts, pictures, notes, and so on—**Selecting Objects**

Selecting multiple fields in a database form

You don't need to switch to **list view** to select more than one **field**. If you point at the **form's** background and begin dragging, Works displays a dotted rectangle. Drag until you surround the fields you want to select. When you release the mouse button, all the enclosed fields are selected.

Selecting Cells

To select a single cell, click it or use the direction keys to move the **cell selector**, a heavy border that indicates the **active cell**.

To select a rectangular **range** of cells, drag the mouse from one corner of the range to the opposite corner. With the keyboard, move the active cell to one corner of the range, hold down the Shift key, and use the direction keys to move to the opposite corner. When you select a range, one cell—the one that is outlined but not reversed—is still the active cell.

A mouse shortcut for selecting a range

To quickly select a range of cells, click the cell in one corner of the range. Then hold down the Shift key and click the cell in the opposite corner.

 Selecting Columns and Rows

Selecting Columns and Rows 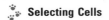 Click a **column** letter or **row** number to select an entire column or row. (In database **list view**, click the **field name** or **record** number.) To select multiple columns or rows, drag from the first column letter or row number in the range you want to select to the last one.

Extending the selection

After you select a cell, a range, a row, or a column, you can extend the selection to adjacent cells by holding the Shift key and pressing a direction key.

⁘ **Selecting Cells**

Selecting Objects  The easiest way to select an object—an embedded **chart, table, Note-It** note, **ClipArt Gallery** picture, what have you—is to click anywhere within the object. You'll know it's selected because it gains a gray border with little squares (called sizing handles) in each corner and along each side. When the object is selected, you can move it, copy it, change its size, or delete it.

Once is enough

Use a single click to select an object. Double-clicking activates the object's source application so you can edit or "play" the object. (Whether a double-click edits or plays depends on the type of object, and is determined by the object's source.)

⁘ **Copying Objects and Pictures; Deleting Objects; Moving Objects and Pictures; Resizing Objects and Pictures**

Selecting Text

 Selecting text in a word processor document is most easily done with a mouse, as shown in the following table.

To select	Do this
A word	Double-click the word
A line	Click in the left margin
A sentence	Hold Ctrl and click within the sentence
A paragraph	Double-click in the left margin
Entire document	Hold Ctrl and click in the left margin

If you prefer the keyboard, simply place the **insertion point** where you want to begin the selection, hold down Shift, and use direction keys to extend the selection.

Extending the selection

To select more than one word, line, sentence, or paragraph, take the action shown in the table above and then, without releasing the mouse button, drag to include adjacent words, lines, sentences, or paragraphs.

Sending and Receiving Files

 You can send a document (or any other type of file stored on your computer) to another computer. Similarly, you can receive a file sent from the other computer and save it directly to a disk file instead of having it appear in the document window.

Before you send or receive a file, find out what **protocol** the other computer uses, and set yours to match. Then make a connection with the other computer.

Sending a File

1 Choose the Tools Send File command.

2 When the Send File dialog box appears, select the drive, directory, and filename of the file you want to send.

3 Choose OK.

Works signals the other computer that it's ready to begin sending a file and displays a dialog box that shows its progress. To stop a file transfer before it's finished, press Esc.

continues

S

Sending and Receiving Files *(continued)*

Receiving a File

1 Ask the operator of the other computer—or the other computer itself—to begin sending a file. With most online services, you initiate a file transfer by selecting a file to "download" and then sending a command that tells the other computer to begin the download.

2 Choose the Tools Receive File command.

3 The Receive File dialog box appears. If you are using the Xmodem protocol, type a filename and choose OK. (With the other protocols, Works automatically saves the files with the same name used on the original system.)

Works displays its progress in the Receive File dialog box. To cancel a file transfer before it's finished, press Esc.

 Sending and Receiving Text

Sending and Receiving Text When you send or receive text, it appears in the document window without any formatting. To send text after you've made a connection, you simply type. The text you type should appear on your screen and on the other computer's screen.

Sending Text from Another Document

If you want to send large chunks of text that you've already typed somewhere else, such as in another document, follow these steps:

1 In the other document, select the text you want to send.

2 Choose Edit Copy to copy the text to the **Clipboard**.

3 Switch to the communications document.

4 Choose the Edit Paste Text command.

Works sends the text to the other computer. And it does it a lot faster than I can type.

Sending Text from a File

You can also send text that has been saved in an **ASCII text file.**
Connect to the other computer and then follow these steps:

1 Choose the Tools Send Text command.

2 Select the name of the file that contains the text you want to send.

3 Choose OK.

What's the difference between "sending text" and "sending files"?

When I talk about sending or receiving text, I'm referring to the stuff that appears in the communications document's window, which is usually unformatted text. Unless you capture it to a file, this information disappears forever when you close the communications document.

Files that you send or receive, on the other hand, don't appear in the document window. They go directly between your disk and the other computer's disk. Although this type of file transfer is commonly used for **binary files**, you can send or receive any type of file this way.

 Capturing Text; Sending and Receiving Files

Series

 Charts

Shading  To add background shading to spreadsheet **cells** or to database **fields, field names**, labels, or **forms**, follow these steps:

1 Select the cells or fields that you want to color. (If you want to shade the background of a database form, click in the background so that no field is selected.)

2 Choose the Format Patterns command.

continues

143

Shading *(continued)*

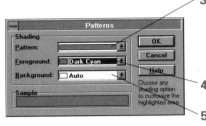

3 For a solid-colored background, select the solid bar in the Pattern list box (the first choice below None). Or select a **pattern**.

4 Select a color from the Foreground list.

5 If you selected a nonsolid pattern, you can select a background color.

6 Choose OK.

The colors you select are applied to the pattern you select from the Pattern list—not to the text in the selection.

What color is Auto?

The Auto color option uses colors that you set in Windows Control Panel. The Window Text color is used as foreground, and the Window Background color is used as, um, background.

 Color; Protecting Form Designs

Sharing Works Data  You can embed Works spreadsheets or **charts** into other applications that use **object linking and embedding** (OLE), such as Microsoft Word or WordPerfect for Windows. Follow these steps:

1 Select the spreadsheet **range** or chart you want to use.

2 Choose the Edit Copy command.

3 Switch to your other application and display the document you want to add the Works data to.

4 Use the other application's Edit Paste or Edit Paste Special command to embed the spreadsheet or chart in the document.

Clipboard; Exporting Documents

Sorting Records

You can sort database **records** based on the contents of up to three fields. You might use this to arrange records in ZIP order before performing a **mail merge** or just to change the order for viewing. To do so, choose the Tools Sort Records command.

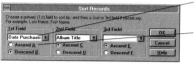

Select the name of the field you want to sort on.

Select the sort order: ascending (A to Z, lowest to highest, first to last) or descending (the other way!).

The Tools Sort Record command sorts the entire database, including hidden records.

Sorting records for reports

You don't need to use the Tools Sort Records command to produce a sorted report. The report generator can sort (and also group) records when it prepares a report.

Finding Records; Reports; Queries

Sorting Rows

You can sort the rows of a spreadsheet—or part of a spreadsheet—by choosing the Tools Sort Rows command. Follow these steps:

1 Select the rows you want to sort. (Works always sorts entire rows, even if you select only partial rows.)
2 Choose the Tools Sort Rows command.
3 Type the letter of the column you want to sort on.
4 Select the sort order: ascending or descending.
5 Repeat steps 3 and 4 to sort on additional columns.
6 Choose OK.

Selecting Columns and Rows

Special Characters

The Insert Special Character command inserts a code to print some variable information, such as the current page number, the name of the document file, or the date you print a document. These codes appear in your document as a word between a pair of asterisks, but notice that Works treats the entire word as a single character, which you can format, copy, and move like any other. When you print the document, Works replaces the code with the appropriate information.

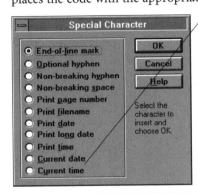

Special Character
◉ End-of-line mark
○ Optional hyphen
○ Non-breaking hyphen
○ Non-breaking space
○ Print page number
○ Print filename
○ Print date
○ Print long date
○ Print time
○ Current date
○ Current time

OK
Cancel
Help

Select the character to insert and choose OK.

The Insert Special Character command also provides a fast way to insert the current date or current time in a document.

But wait. There's more!

You can use the Insert Special Character command to insert **nonprinting characters**. If you use any of them frequently, you'll quickly learn its keyboard shortcut, which provides a faster, easier way to insert them.

To insert this character	You can use this shortcut key
End-of-line mark	Shift+Enter
Optional hyphen	Ctrl+hyphen
Nonbreaking hyphen	Ctrl+Shift+hyphen
Nonbreaking space	Ctrl+Shift+Spacebar

ANSI Characters; Ending Lines; Hyphenation; Nonbreaking Spaces

Spelling Checker

Works can check documents for misspelled words. To use the spelling checker, first select the text or **cells** you want to proof. (If you want to proof an entire document, don't select any text or select a single cell.) Then choose the Tools Spelling command. Works pauses when it finds a word that's not in its dictionary and displays the Spelling dialog box.

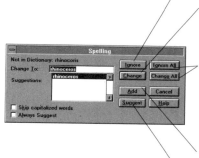

Choose Ignore if the word is, in fact, correct and you want Works to continue looking for other errors.

Choose Change to replace the misspelled word with the contents of the Change To box.

Choose Ignore All or Change All to tell Works to ignore or change other occurrences of the word instead of stopping to ask about each one.

Choose Add if you want Works to add the word to its dictionary.

Choose Suggest to have Works look for similar words in its dictionary. (Mark the Always Suggest check box if you want Works to automatically make suggestions.)

Selecting a Dictionary

Dictionaries are available for other languages and for specialized vocabularies, such as legalese. To select a dictionary that's been installed on your system, choose the Tools Options command. Then select a dictionary from the Speller list.

continues

Spelling Checker *(continued)*

Checking databases and spreadsheets

In a database, the spelling checker proofs only the contents of the database **records**. It's up to you to find errors in **field names**, labels, or other text on database **forms**. The spelling checker also ignores cells and **fields** that contain **formulas**.

Spreadsheets

A spreadsheet is a document type that was inspired by accountants' ruled ledger forms. In its electronic rendition, a spreadsheet is a huge grid of **cells** in which you can enter numbers or **formulas** that perform calculations on the **values** in other cells.

⋮ **New Documents**

Spreadsheet View

When you are viewing a **chart**, you can switch back to the spreadsheet on which the chart is based by choosing the View Spreadsheet command. To switch to spreadsheet view from a chart embedded in a word processor document or database **form**, follow these steps:

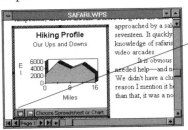

1 Double-click the chart to activate it.

2 Click the spreadsheet icon to switch to spreadsheet view. You can then modify the numbers that create the chart.

⋮ **Views**

S

Starting Works
You start Works by double-clicking the Microsoft Works icon in Program Manager's Microsoft Works for Windows program group. Follow these steps:

Microsoft Works

1 If Microsoft Windows isn't already running, start it by typing *win* at the MS-DOS prompt.

2 In Program Manager, choose the Window Microsoft Works For Windows command to open the Works program group.

3 Double-click the Microsoft Works icon.

The first time you start Works, the Welcome To Microsoft Works dialog box appears—offering you an opportunity to take a guided tour of Works. If you don't want to be bothered by this dialog box in the future, choose the Skip Welcome Screen button.

 Options; Saving the Workspace; Startup Dialog Box

Startup Dialog Box
The Startup dialog box is your "control center" for Microsoft Works. It lets you create a new **document**, open an existing document, or use a **template** or **WorksWizard**. To open the Startup dialog box, do one of the following:

- Start Works (unless you have saved the **workspace**, in which case Works displays the saved workspace instead).

- Click the Startup Dialog tool.

- Choose the File Create New File command.

- Choose the File WorksWizards command.

- Choose the File Templates command.

- Close the only open **document window**.

It's the same everywhere you look

No matter how you open the Startup dialog box, you can access all the same features. The only difference you'll encounter by opening it with different commands is which button is initially selected.

Statistical Functions Works has seven statistical functions, which calculate the sum, average (mean), number, minimum or maximum value, standard deviation, or variance of a group of numbers. **Arguments** in the statistical functions can be **values** or cell references (including **range** addresses or **names**); separate the arguments with a comma. The following **formula** produces the sum of the values in each of the specified cells:

=SUM(B1:B12)

That's sum button

The easiest way to insert a formula that calculates the sum of a column or row of numbers is to click the **AutoSum** tool.

> **Absolute Cell References; Mixed Cell References; Relative Cell References**

Status Bar The status bar appears at the bottom of the Works **application window**. At its left end is a message area that describes each command as you highlight it.

The right end of the status bar shows information about the active **document**. When a word processor document is active, Works shows the number of the current page and the total number of pages. For a **database**, Works displays the number of the current **record**, the number of nonhidden records, and the total number of records in the database. During a communications session, Works displays the amount of time you've been connected.

Sandwiched in between are several indicators:

Indicator	What it means
CAPS	The keyboard's Caps Lock is on, which means that all letter keys type as capitals. Press the Caps Lock key to turn Caps Lock off.
NUM	The keyboard's Num Lock is on, which means the numeric keypad enters numbers. If you want to use its direction keys, hold down Shift. Or you can press the Num Lock key to turn Num Lock off.
OVR	Overtype mode is selected, which means that each character you type replaces the character to the right of the **insertion point**. To turn overtype mode off, press the Ins key.
CIRC	The spreadsheet contains a **circular reference**.
OFFLINE	You are not connected to another computer.
DIAL	The modem is making a connection.
PLAY	A recorded script is playing back.
REC	You are currently recording a communications script.

What status bar?

If your Works window doesn't have a status bar, choose the Tools Options command and then mark the Show Status Bar check box.

Subtotaling Records  To perform calculations on groups of related database records, create a report.

   Reports; Report View

Switching Windows

Microsoft Windows and Works provide an ideal environment for people who like to jump from one fleeting thought to another because you don't need to finish one activity before you start something else. You can make any window the active window by clicking in it, or you can use one of these keystrokes:

To activate the next	Press
Window pane	F6
Document window	Ctrl+F6 or Ctrl+Tab
Application window	Alt+Tab

Synonyms

Thesaurus

Tables

A table in a word processor document is actually a Works **spreadsheet** in disguise. This has its advantages: Unlike ordinary tabular text, Works tables can perform calculations. (Of course, your table doesn't have to contain numeric information.) And if you know how to use the Works spreadsheet module, you know everything there is to know about using tables.

Creating a Table

To create a table in a word processor document, follow these steps:

1 Place the **insertion point** where you want the table.

2 Choose the Insert Spreadsheet/Table command.

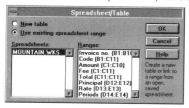

3 If you want to create a new table, select the New Table radio button and choose OK. (You can instead insert a **range** from a spreadsheet. To do that, you must save the spreadsheet, have the spreadsheet document open, and give a **name** to the range you want to use.)

4 Works embeds a small spreadsheet in your document.

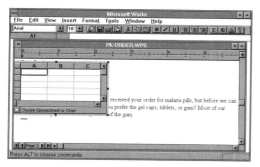

You can enter text or numbers in the spreadsheet. Notice that, while the spreadsheet is active, the spreadsheet toolbar and menus appear. (The spreadsheet is active when it displays row numbers and column letters, and has a thick border and scroll bars.)

continues

Tables *(continued)*

Modifying a Table

To activate an embedded spreadsheet (table), double-click it. Click outside the spreadsheet to return to the word processor text.

If you need to change the number of columns or rows, drag the sizing handles (the little squares along the spreadsheet's border) to enlarge or reduce the spreadsheet.

You can adjust the **column width** or **row height** by dragging the border of the column letter or row number that you want to change.

 Borders

Tabs

In Works, you can create different tab-stop settings in each **paragraph**. Even if you don't set any tab stops in a paragraph, Works uses its own default tab stops, which are normally set every half inch.

The **ruler** shows the tab-stop settings for the current paragraph (the one containing the **insertion point**) using these symbols:

Left (left aligns text)   Right (right aligns text)

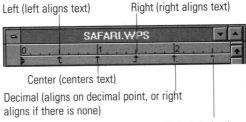

Center (centers text)

Decimal (aligns on decimal point, or right aligns if there is none)

Default (left aligns text)

Setting Tab Stops

1 Select the paragraph(s) in which you want to set tab stops.

2 Choose the Format Tabs command.

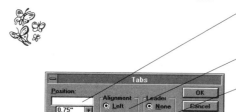

3 Type the position of the tab stop you want to add.

4 Select an alignment radio button.

5 Select a leader radio button if you want a dotted line or other character to fill the blank space before the tab stop.

6 Choose the Insert button.

7 Repeat steps 3 through 6 to set additional tab stops. Choose OK when you're finished.

Using Tabs

Press the Tab key to insert a tab character, which moves the insertion point to the next tab stop, leaving a blank space in its wake.

Changing tab stops with the ruler and the mouse

To insert a left tab stop, click the ruler where you want the tab stop. To insert a tab stop with any other alignment (or with a leader character), double-click the ruler to display the Tabs dialog box.

To move an existing tab stop, drag it along the ruler to its new location.

To delete a tab stop, drag it off the ruler.

Nonprinting Characters; Page Tabs

Templates A template is a document that already has some information and formatting in it. When you create a new document, a template gives you a head start compared with starting from a blank screen. Works comes with several templates, and you can easily modify them or create your own.

Creating a Template

1 Create the document you want to use as a template. (A blank letterhead or expense report, perhaps?)

2 Choose the File Save As command.

3 Choose the Template button.

4 Type a name for your template and choose OK.

Works adds your template to the Custom template group.

Using a Template

1 Choose the File Templates command.

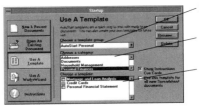

2 Select a template group.

3 Select a template category.

4 Select a template.

5 Choose OK.

Assigning a default template

You can select a template for each Works module (word processor, spreadsheet, database, and communications) to use as a default template, which means that Works uses that template whenever you create a new document. In the Use A Template dialog box, select the template you want to use as the default. Then mark the Use This Template For All New *Module* Documents check box before you choose OK.

: **AutoStart Templates; Saving Documents; WorksWizards**

T

Terminal Settings The options in the Terminal Settings
dialog box control how Works displays text it receives
from another computer. To access this dialog box, choose
the Settings Terminal command.

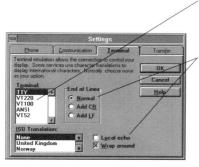

If the other computer
expects you to have a
specific type of terminal,
select it here.

If text transmitted in a
communications session
overlaps, is double-
spaced, or doesn't appear
at all, tinker with the End
Of Lines, Local Echo, and
Wrap Around settings.
(See the Troubleshooting
section for more
information.)

Communication Settings; Phone Settings; Protocol

Text Columns To format your document into two or
more newspaper-style columns, choose the Format Columns command.

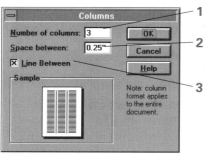

1 Type the number of
columns you want.

2 Type the amount of
blank space to leave
between each column.

3 Mark the Line Be-
tween check box if you
want a vertical line to
print between each
column.

4 Choose OK.

To see the result of your change, choose the View Page Layout
command or use **print preview**.

Text Functions

Microsoft Works includes 16 **functions** that, unlike all the other Works functions, operate on text instead of numeric **values**. With these text functions, you can format text with uniform capitalization, extract some text from a text string, remove blank spaces, and more. The following **formula** converts the text in cell B2 so that the first letter of each word is uppercase and all other letters are lowercase:

=PROPER(B2)

Arguments in a text function can be **cell addresses** or a text string enclosed in quotation marks, like this:

=EXACT("Match this!",B2)

(This formula returns TRUE if cell B2 contains the text *Match this!*, or FALSE if it contains anything else.)

Text String Formulas

Text String Formulas

Formulas that operate on text strings can use **text functions** and they can use the & operator, which joins two text strings. In the illustration below, cell A4 contains the formula:

=PROPER(A2)&", "&UPPER(LEFT(B2,2))

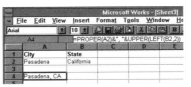

This formula ensures that the city name (cell A2) is capitalized properly, appends a comma and a space, and then appends the capitalized first two letters of the state name (B2).

Thesaurus The thesaurus provides synonyms when you can't think of the right (correct, proper, perfect) word (expression, statement, locution). To use the thesaurus in Works, follow these steps:

1 Select the word for which you want to find a synonym.

2 Choose the Tools Thesaurus command.

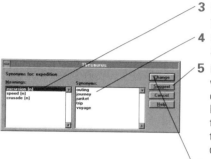

3 Select the meaning you're looking for.

4 Select a word in the Synonyms list box.

5 If you're not satisfied with the choices, choose Suggest to look up synonyms for the word you select in the Meanings or Synonyms list.

6 Choose Change to replace your original word with the word you select in the Meanings or Synonyms list.

Time Formats Using decimal values to represent times is useful for performing calculations, but if you want to see the **time values** in a format you can read (that is, a format that is recognizable as a time), follow these steps:

1 Select the cells that contain a time value.

2 Choose the Format Number command.

3 In the Format box, select the Time radio button.

4 In the Options box, select the format you want: 12-hour or 24-hour format, with or without seconds.

 **Formatting Numbers**

Times  To insert the current time or the time when a document prints into a word processor document, choose the Insert Special Character command.

☙ **Special Characters**

Time Values Works uses decimal values to represent times, where each whole number represents 24 hours. 0 (or any whole number) represents 12:00 A.M., 0.25 represents 6:00 A.M., 0.5 represents 12:00 noon, and so on. This feature lets you perform calculations on time values (finding the elapsed time between two events, for example).

☙ **Formulas; Time Formats**

Toolbars 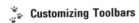 The toolbar is the row of graphical buttons right near the top of the Works **application window**. Clicking a toolbar button (a tool) is a shortcut for choosing a command from a menu. The toolbar changes depending on what type of **document window** is active. To turn the toolbar display off (or back on), choose the View Toolbar command.

Slow down and it'll come to you

Some of the icons used on toolbar buttons don't exactly promote instant recognition. In fact, there's no telling what they are. But if you move the mouse pointer to a toolbar button and wait a few seconds, a Tool Tip appears that tells what the tool does.

☙ **Customizing Toolbars**

Transfer Settings

> ∴ **Protocol**

TrueType

TrueType refers to the font-scaling technology in Microsoft Windows. TrueType **fonts** appear the same on the screen and on the printed page, and can be scaled (enlarged or reduced) to almost any size. To use TrueType fonts, look for the ⊤ icon next to the font name in the list of fonts.

Underline Characters

To <u>underline</u> characters, select the text (or the cells that contain the text) and then press Ctrl+U or click the Underline tool.

Undo

The Edit Undo command is the "Oops!" command. If you format some text, for example, and then decide that Wingdings is not a very legible font after all, choose Edit Undo. The Undo command can undo only your last action, so you must choose it before you make any other changes to your document.

> ∴ **Redo**

Values

A value is a number that you enter in a **cell** or a **formula**, and which can be used in arithmetic calculations performed by other formulas. Strictly speaking, a value can contain only digits (0 through 9), a decimal point (period), and a sign (+ or −). You can also use formatting characters (such as a dollar sign, comma, or percent sign), but Works doesn't retain them as part of the actual value.

> ∴ **Formatting Numbers; Percentages; Scientific Notation**

Views   Each Works module offers several ways to look at a document. To change views, choose the name of the view you want from the View menu, or click the appropriate **toolbar** button.

	Draft	Fast but ugly; doesn't display actual fonts and displays embedded objects as empty rectangles
	Normal	Compromise between speed and beauty; shows objects and actual fonts, but not in position
	Page Layout	Slower than normal view; shows everything in position—like **print preview**—except you can edit
	Wrap for Window	Changes line endings to fit the **document window**; horizontal **scrolling** is unnecessary
	Chart	Shows spreadsheet information in a graphical format
	Spreadsheet	The basics: numbers on a grid
	Form	Displays a single **record** in a form-like layout
	List	Displays records in a spreadsheet-like window; each record occupies one row
	Query	Displays **query** sentences in a window that looks like form view
	Report	Displays a **report** definition

Zooming

Window Panes

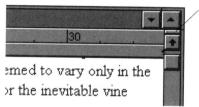

You can split the **document window** for a word processor document, spreadsheet, or database (**list view** only) into two panes, which allows you to look at different parts of the same document. You can scroll the information in each pane independently.

Splitting a Window into Two Panes

Drag the split bar—the tiny gap above the vertical scroll bar—down to divide the window into two panes. Alternatively, choose the Window Split command and click or press Enter when the split bar is where you want it.

Split bar

In spreadsheets and databases, you can split the document window into four panes if you like. These windows have a vertical split bar in addition to the horizontal split bar.

To remove the split and restore a single-pane view, drag the split bar to the edge of the window.

Moving between panes isn't a pain

To place the **insertion point** in a pane, you click there. But you needn't take your hands off the keyboard to move to a different pane: Simply press F6 to move to the next pane.

 Scrolling

WordArt

WordArt is an accessory application that lets you create wacky distorted text. You can use it to create a logo or a heading in a word processor document or database **form**.

continues

163

WordArt *(continued)*

Creating a WordArt Object

1 Place the **insertion point** where you want the WordArt object to appear, and then choose the Insert WordArt command.

2 WordArt displays a new Enter Your Text Here window. Type the text that you want to use in your WordArt.

3 Choose the shape, font, and other effects you want using the WordArt **toolbar** and menu commands.

4 Choose the Update Display button. If you don't like what you see, go back to step 3.

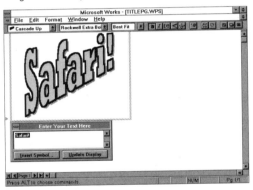

5 To close the Enter Your Text Here window, double-click its control-menu icon or click anywhere else in the **document window**.

❖ **Moving Objects and Pictures; Object Linking and Embedding; Resizing Objects and Pictures**

WordPerfect 📎 WordPerfect is a word processor that's used by more people than the combined population of the countries of middle Africa. You can exchange documents with users of WordPerfect versions 5.0, 5.1, and 5.2 because Works can open and save documents in those formats.

❖ **Exporting Documents; Opening Documents; Saving Documents**

Word Wrap Word wrap is the feature that moves a word to the next line when it doesn't fit on the current line. It might not sound like much—until you have an older person explain how typewriters worked in the olden days.

Doin' the word wrap

Normally Works wraps words based on the length of printed lines. In other words, your document appears on screen as it will when you print it. If you can't see complete lines on the screen, use the **zooming** feature to display more of the document or choose the View Wrap For Window command. Works then breaks lines to fit in the screen window—without affecting the way lines break when printed.

> **Ending Lines**

Workspace The workspace is the part of the Works **application window** below the **toolbar**—the area where **document windows** appear.

> **Saving the Workspace**

WorksWizards WorksWizards are helpers that can assist you in creating specialized databases, finding files, and other common tasks. They do so by asking you a series of questions (and showing by example what different answers will produce) and then performing all the necessary steps to complete the task. To use a WorksWizard (and to see a list and descriptions of the available wizards), choose File WorksWizards.

> **Address Book WorksWizard; File Organizer WorksWizard; Form Letter WorksWizard; Templates**

Write   Write is a word processor that's included with Microsoft Windows. Because every Windows user has a copy, its format is convenient for exchanging documents with other users who don't have Works. But you don't have to use Write. Works can open and save word processor documents in Write format; simply choose Windows Write from the file-type list when you open or save a document.

Exporting Documents; Opening Documents; Saving Documents

Zooming   Like a camera's zoom lens, Works can "zoom in" to give you a magnified view of the active document. Zooming enlarges or reduces the size of characters on the display, but it does not affect printed output. To zoom, choose the View Zoom command.

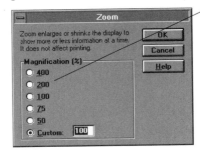

Select a magnification factor from the list, or type a custom magnification from 25% through 1000% of normal size.

Print Preview; Views

TROUBLE-
SHOOTING

Got a problem? Starting on the next page are solutions to the problems that can plague users of Microsoft Works for Windows. You'll be on your way—and safely out of danger—in no time.

COMMUNICATIONS

You Can't Access
a Modem

If Works displays a message such as "COM2 Port already in use," it means that another program is using the modem or you've selected the wrong **COM port** for your modem.

Close other communications programs

1 If you have an active connection in another Works communications document, switch to its window and choose the Phone Hang Up command.

2 Be sure you aren't using another program that's accessing the modem, such as a phone dialer or a program that checks your remote electronic mail or tracks overnight package deliveries. Close such a program.

Check your modem setup

1 Choose the Settings Modem command and then choose the Test button. Works tests each COM port in your system and finds which ones have a modem attached.

2 If the modem test finds a modem on a different port than the error message reported, choose Settings Communications and select the port found by the modem test.

 Communications Settings; Modem Setup

The Communications
Window Displays
"Garbage"

Don't take offense if the text in the communications window looks like a cartoon-character expletive.

Match the communication settings

1 Find out from the operator of the online service or computer you want to connect to what communications settings (baud rate, data bits, parity, and stop bits) to use.

2 Choose Settings Communication and set each item to match the other computer.

 Communications Settings

The Text in the Communications Document Window Isn't Right

Most systems that you connect to use similar conventions about which characters they send to your terminal, how they handle line endings, and so on. But not all of them. Choose the Settings Terminal command to solve the following problems.

If lines overprint or are double spaced

If each new line of text in a communications window displays right over the previous line, select Add LF in the End Of Lines box.

If a blank line appears between each line of text, select Normal in the End Of Lines box.

Characters appear twice or not at all

If every character you type appears twice, clear the Local Echo check box. If characters you type don't appear at all, mark the Local Echo check box.

Characters overprint at right end

If characters "pile up" at the right end of the line, mark the Wrap Around check box.

 Terminal Settings

Pasting Text Doesn't Work

Sometimes when you choose Edit Paste Text to send text from the Clipboard, the other computer can't keep up—and it doesn't correctly receive all the text.

Increase the line delay

1 Choose the Settings Transfer command.

2 Increase the number in the Line Delay box, which represents the time (in tenths of a second) that Works pauses at the end of each line to give the other computer a chance to catch its breath.

 Sending and Receiving Text

DATABASE

You Can't Change the Field Entries in a Database

Works lets you protect certain fields from changes. (This is especially handy for protecting a field that contains a formula, for example.) But if you're sure you want to change the contents of a protected field, you can.

Remove data protection

To remove protection from all fields, choose Format Protection and clear the Protect Data check box.

If you want to remove protection from a certain field without endangering other fields, follow these steps:

1 Select the field(s) you want to unprotect.

2 Choose Format Protection.

3 Clear the Locked check box and choose OK.

 Protecting Cells and Fields

You Can't Make Changes to a Database

When a database **form** is protected, Works also prevents you from making many changes in **list view. Adding fields** and **formatting numbers** is prohibited, and you can't change **field names**, add **headers and footers**, or have any other fun.

Remove form protection

1 Choose View Form to switch to **form view**.

2 Choose Format Protection.

3 Clear the Protect Form check box and choose OK.

 Protecting Form Designs

East Coast ZIP Codes Lose Their Leading Zero

Normally, Works drops zeros at the beginning of a number. But in some cases, such as for ZIP codes, those zeros are significant.

Use leading zero format

1 Select the field you want to format.

2 Choose the Format Number command.

3 Select Leading Zeros and enter a Number Of Digits. (Use 5 for a ZIP code.)

 Formatting Numbers

FILES

You Get a GPF When You Try to Open Any File

I know, it sounds wacky. But if you get a General Protection Fault (a terrible, terrible error affectionately known as a GPF) whenever you try to open a file, you could have a corrupt printer driver.

Change printer drivers

If you have another printer driver installed, use Control Panel to select it and then restart Works. If everything works, you'll thank me and wonder how I knew. (I'm not telling.) To avoid the problem in the future (or if you don't have another driver installed), follow these steps:

1 Start Control Panel (in Program Manager's Main group) and double-click the Printers icon.

2 Select the printer driver that causes the error and choose Remove. (Yes, you're sure.)

3 Choose the Add button, select your printer model from the List Of Printers, and choose Install.

You Can't Find a Document File

If you move or delete a file and then select it in the Recently Used Files list in the **Startup dialog box**, Works reports that it can't find the file.

Use a WorksWizard

If the file has been deleted, you might be out of luck. Try the Undelete program that comes with MS-DOS versions 5 and later. But the longer it's been since the deletion, the less likely you'll be successful. For more information—if you'll excuse some shameless self-promotion—look in the *Field Guide to MS-DOS 6.2* (Microsoft Press, 1994).

If the file has been renamed or moved to another directory, use the **File Organizer WorksWizard** to find it.

You Can't Open a Document File

Works does not allow a document to be open in more than one window or to be open by more than one person at a time.

Split the window

If you already have a document open in another Works window and you're trying to view different parts of the same document, split the window into two panes instead of trying to open a second document window.

Close the open document

If you want to open a document that's already open in another application on your computer or open by someone on another computer, you'll have to close the document before you can open it in Works.

 Closing Documents; Window Panes

PRINTING

Pages Don't Break Where You Want

Works considers several factors when it decides where to put page breaks: page size, **page orientation, margins**, restrictions on **paragraph breaks**, and manual **page breaks** that you insert.

Insert a manual page break

1 Place the insertion point (or select the row or column) where you want a page break.

2 Choose the Insert Page Break command.

Save a tree!

To find out where pages break without wasting paper, choose Print Preview.

The Printout Uses the Wrong Font and Graphics Don't Print

Works has a nifty feature that lets you print faster by avoiding font changes and not printing graphics. This feature can cause dismay if it's not what you expect, however.

Don't use the draft printing feature

Choose the File Print command and clear the Draft Quality Printing check box.

Field Placeholders Print Instead of Merge Data

To merge information from a database into a word processor document, you insert a placeholder—the field name surrounded by « and » symbols—in the document. But that's not what you want to see when you print.

Use the print merge feature

Choose the File Print command and mark the Print Merge check box.

 Mail Merge

Only Part of a Spreadsheet Prints

The print area is set incorrectly. Change the print area to the entire spreadsheet.

Reset the print area

1 Choose Edit Select All.

2 Choose Format Set Print Area.

You Can't Get Gridlines to Print

Gridlines—those lines that separate the **cells** in a spreadsheet or **fields** in database **list view** —can be prevented from displaying and printing. But the View Gridlines command, which controls the display, does not affect printing.

Change the page setup

1 Choose the File Page Setup command and select the Other Options tab.

2 Mark the Print Gridlines check box if you want gridlines to print; clear it if you don't.

Charts Don't Print in Color

The default printer that's selected when you place a **chart** in a word processor document determines how the chart will preview and print. If the default printer is a black-and-white printer, you won't be able to print in color, even if you switch to a color printer.

Select a color printer first

Select a color printer as the default printer and then re-create the chart.

SPREADSHEETS AND TABLES

Formulas Don't Calculate Correctly

If a **formula** doesn't calculate the way you expect it to, it's probably a matter of "operator precedence," which means that certain operators (an operator, such as a plus sign, specifies what Works should do with the values on either side) are evaluated first—no matter where they occur in a formula. You can control the order of calculation with parentheses: Enclose the part of a formula that you want to calculate first within parentheses.

Works Doesn't Recognize Your Entry as a Formula

If you enter a **formula** and Works displays the formula in the cell instead of the **value** produced by the formula, you probably forgot one little thing: You must start each formula with an equal sign (=).

Edit the formula

1 Select the formula that's not a formula.

2 Press F2 to jump to the formula bar.

3 Press the Home key to move to the beginning of the formula, type an equal sign, and press Enter.

You Can't Enter Anything into a Cell

Works lets you protect certain cells from changes, which is handy for protecting formulas. But if you're sure you want to change the contents of a protected cell, you can.

Remove data protection

To remove protection from all cells, choose Format Protection and clear the Protect Data check box.

If you want to remove protection from a certain cell without affecting other cells, follow these steps:

1 Select the cell(s) you want to unprotect.

2 Choose Format Protection.

3 Clear the Locked check box and choose OK.

 Protecting Cells and Fields

You Can't Display Long Text Entries

If a label or text entry won't fit within a column, Works lets it spread into adjacent cells on the right—until it runs into a cell that isn't empty.

Increase the column width

Double-click the column letter or field name to adjust the **column width** to fit the text.

Wrap the text onto multiple lines

1 Select the cell that won't fit.

2 Choose the Format Alignment command.

3 Mark the Wrap Text check box.

Values Display as

If a number or date is too wide to fit in a column, Works displays pound signs instead. The **value** in the cell is still there (and calculations are not affected); you just can't see it.

Increase the column width

Double-click the column letter or field name to adjust the **column width** to fit the column's contents.

Change the formatting

Select the offending cell and then choose the Format Number command. Select a format that requires less space: Eliminate unnecessary decimal places, commas, dollar signs, and so on. Or select General format.

Alternatively, you can select a smaller font size from the toolbar's point-size drop-down list.

 Formatting Numbers

WORD PROCESSOR

You Can't See Graphics on the Screen

When you insert a picture or other object in a word processor document, it's visible only in certain **views**.

Change the view

Graphics are never visible in draft view. Choose the View Normal command to switch to normal view. If the graphic is still not visible, choose View Page Layout.

Change the text-wrap options

If the graphic is visible only in page layout view, and you don't need to have text on either side of it, follow these steps:

1 Choose View Page Layout.
2 Select the graphic.
3 Choose Format Picture/Object and select the Text Wrap tab.
4 Select the In-Line Wrap button and choose OK.

QUICK REFERENCE

Any time you explore some exotic location, you're bound to see flora and fauna you can't identify. To make sure you can identify the toolbar buttons you see in Microsoft Works, the Quick Reference describes these items in systematic detail.

File Menu Tools

 Prints the active document

 Shows what the printed pages will look like

 Displays the Startup dialog box, which lets you create a new document, open an existing document, or use a template or WorksWizard

 Opens an existing document

 Saves the active document

 Runs the File Organizer WorksWizard, which finds documents in any drive or directory

Sends the active document as an e-mail or fax message

Edit Menu Tools

 Undoes the last change

 Cuts the selection from the document and moves it to the Clipboard

 Copies the selection from the document to the Clipboard

 Pastes the Clipboard contents into the active document

 Deletes the selection without changing the Clipboard contents

What? No toolbar?

If your Works display doesn't include a toolbar right below the menu bar, choose the View Toolbar command.

🔍	Finds text in the active document	📖 📑 📑
📋	Jumps to a specific place in the active document	📖 📑 📑
➡️	Copies values, formats, and formulas from the leftmost selected cells to the selected cells to the right	📑 📑
⬇️	Copies values, formats, and formulas from the topmost selected cells to the selected cells below	📑 📑
📊	Fills selected cells with a series of numbers or dates	📑 📑
📋	Edits legend or series labels	📑
📊	Jumps to the first data series in the spreadsheet	📑

Have it your way

Late one night, wired on pizza and soda, the Works programmers voted on their favorite toolbar buttons, and those are the ones included in the default toolbar for each module. This Quick Reference shows *all* the available toolbar buttons. If you find a button here that is not on the default toolbar and that performs an action you use frequently, see **Customizing Toolbars**.

View Menu Tools

📄	Wraps the text to fit in the window	📖
📄	Displays all open word processing documents in draft view	📖
📄	Displays the active document in page layout view	📖
📄	Displays the active document in normal view	📖

continues

View Menu Tools *(continued)*

¶	Shows all nonprinting characters	☞
⊡	Displays the ruler	☞
⊞	Jumps to the spreadsheet when a chart window is active	
⊞	Displays gridlines	
⊡	Displays selection in form view	
⊞	Displays selection in list view	
⊡	Creates a new query or activates the last query	
⊡	Creates a new report or activates the last report	
⊡	Applies an existing query	
⊡	Displays all records	
⊡	Displays hidden records and hides visible records	
⊡	Hides selected records	
⊡	Displays field lines	

Tool Tips are sharp

When you leave the mouse pointer poised over a toolbar button, a little window pops up that tells you what the button does. The little window is called a Tool Tip; if you want to test your iconic memory skills, choose the Tools Customize Toolbar command and deselect Enable Tool Tips. (You can still look to the status bar for a more verbose description.)

Insert Menu Tools

	Inserts a page break	✍ 🖳 🖳
	Inserts a footnote	✍
	Inserts a bookmark	✍
	Inserts a database field	✍
	Inserts the current date	✍
	Inserts the current time	✍
	Creates a chart	✍
	Inserts a Draw drawing	✍ 🖳
	Inserts a Note-It note	✍ 🖳
	Inserts a ClipArt Gallery picture	✍ 🖳
	Inserts a WordArt object	✍ 🖳
	Inserts a table	✍
	Names the selection	🖳
	Inserts a function on the formula bar	🖳
	Inserts the SUM() function	🖳
	Inserts blank rows above the selection	🖳

continues

181

Insert Menu Tools *(continued)*

	Inserts blank columns to the left of the selection	
	Deletes selected rows	
	Deletes selected columns	
	Inserts a blank record in the database	
	Deletes selected records	
	Inserts a field	

Gallery Menu Tools

	Displays data as a simple area chart	
	Displays data as a simple bar chart	
	Displays data as a simple line chart	
	Displays data as a simple pie chart	
	Displays data as a stacked line chart	
	Displays data as a scatter chart	
	Displays data as a radar chart	

Gallery? What Gallery?

The Gallery menu appears only when you select the Chart view in a spreadsheet document. You won't find it when you first open a spreadsheet.

	Displays data as a combination chart	
	Displays data as a 3-D area chart	
	Displays data as a 3-D bar chart	
	Displays data as a 3-D line chart	
	Displays data as a 3-D pie chart	

Format Menu Tools

Arial	Changes the font of the selected text	
12	Changes the point size of the selected text	
B	Makes the selected text bold	
I	Italicizes the selected text	
<u>U</u>	Underlines the selected text	
K	Strikes through the selected text	
x^A	Makes the selected text superscript	

continues

Font-selection tools

The procedure for including the font and point size list boxes on the toolbar is not the same as the procedure for including toolbar buttons. To include them, choose the Tools Customize Toolbar command and deselect "Remove Font Name and Point Size from the toolbar."

Format Menu Tools *(continued)*

![x subscript]	Makes the selected text subscript	✍
![left align]	Aligns selected paragraphs at the left indent	✍ 🖥 🖨
![center]	Centers selected paragraphs between the left and right indents	✍ 🖥 🖨
![right align]	Aligns selected paragraphs at the right indent	✍ 🖥 🖨
![justify]	Aligns selected paragraphs at the left and right indents	✍
![left tab]	Sets a left-aligned tab	✍
![center tab]	Sets a center-aligned tab	✍
![right tab]	Sets a right-aligned tab	✍
![decimal tab]	Sets a decimal-aligned tab	✍
![bulleted list]	Formats the selected paragraphs as a bulleted list	✍
![decrease indent]	Decreases the left indent for the selected paragraphs by one-half inch	✍
![increase indent]	Increases the left indent for the selected paragraphs by one-half inch	✍
![single spacing]	Sets line spacing for the selected paragraphs to one line	✍
![double spacing]	Sets line spacing for the selected paragraphs to two lines	✍
![columns]	Sets the column format for the active document	✍
![position object]	Positions a selected object in-line or by absolute measurement	✍

⬚	Adds a border around the selected paragraphs, cells, or chart	✍ 🖥
⬚	Applies predefined formats to a table	🖥
$	Applies currency format to the selection	🖥
%	Applies percent format to the selection	🖥
,	Applies comma format to the selection	🖥
⊞	Centers cell contents across selected columns	🖥
▨	Changes patterns and colors	🖥
⊞	Freezes rows and columns before the selection as titles	🖥
🔒	Protects data from changes	🖥 🖨
🖎	Sets selected cells as the area to print	🖥
⊞	Aligns fields to a grid	🖨
🗎	Protects the active form from changes	🖨
🗎	Shows the field name	🖨

Settings Menu Tools

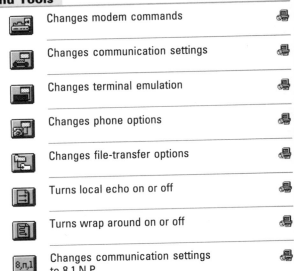

	Changes modem commands
	Changes communication settings
	Changes terminal emulation
	Changes phone options
	Changes file-transfer options
	Turns local echo on or off
	Turns wrap around on or off
8,n,1	Changes communication settings to 8,1,N,P
7,e,1	Changes communication settings to 7,1,E,P

Phone Menu Tools

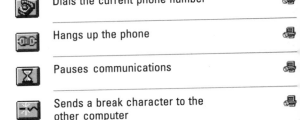

	Dials the current phone number
	Hangs up the phone
	Pauses communications
	Sends a break character to the other computer

Tools Menu Tools

Checks spelling of the selection	
Finds synonyms for the selected word	
Counts the words in the selection	
Creates envelopes or mailing labels	
Dials the selected number	
Displays the Learning Works dialog box, which lets you display Cue Cards, access online help, start the tutorial, or use a WorksWizard	
Creates a chart	
Calculates formulas in the active document	
Sorts records in ascending order	
Sorts records in descending order	
Captures incoming text in a file	
Sends a file	
Sends a document as a binary file	
Receives a binary file	
Records your actions as a script	

Window Menu Tools

 Arranges the open windows in an overlapping cascade

 Arranges the open windows in nonoverlapping tiles

 Places the icons for minimized windows at the bottom of the workspace

SPECIAL CHARACTERS

in cell or field 176
$ (dollar sign) 16, 51, 102
= (equal sign) 64, 83
& operator 158
* wildcard 123
? wildcard 123
« and ». *See* fields, placeholders
» (page break indicator) 110

A

absolute cell references 16
active cell 16
adding fields 16–17, 120, 170
adding pictures 18
adding records 18
Address Book WorksWizard 19
alignment 20, 92
annotations 106
ANSI characters 21, 77
application windows 4–5, 21
arguments 22, 85–86
ASCII text files 22, 69
auto answer 115
Auto color 144
AutoFormat 23
Auto spacing 95
AutoStart templates 23
AutoSum tool 24, 150
Avery labels 98
axis 31

B

background patterns ... 114, 143–44
baud rate 46
beginning of document,
    moving to 138
binary files 24

bold characters .... x, 24, 30
bookmarks 24–25, 86
borders 25–26, 32, 34
buffer 28
bulleted lists 26–27
bullets 21
    See also bulleted lists

C

calculating formulas 27, 83, 100,
    160, 174
calculation order 116
CAPS message 151
capturing text 28
cells
    about 29
    active 16
    address 29
    editing 60–61
    filling 73
    finding 75
    naming 84
    pointer 29
    protecting 119, 175
    references 16, 102, 125
    replacing contents 126
    selecting 139
    selector 29
center alignment 20
centimeters 94
changing fonts 29–31
Character Map application 21
charts
    about 9, 33
    axis 31
    borders 32, 34
    colors 32
    creating 33–36, 41
    editing 61
    fonts 31
    formatting 31–33
    gridlines 32, 34

charts *(continued)*
  labels 37, 39–40
  legends 37, 38
  linking 37
  markers 33
  naming 35
  printing 32, 174
  series 35
  titles 34, 37–38
  types 40–41
check boxes 57
CHOOSE() function 96
CIRC message 42, 151
circular reference 42
ClipArt Gallery 18, 42–43
Clipboard 43–44, 53, 114
closing documents 44
colors
  background 143–44
  charts 32
  text 30
columns
  about 44
  deleting 55
  inserting................................... 93
  selecting 140
  width 45
COM ports 46
comma-separated text 69
communications
  about 12–13
  making a connection 60
  problems......................... 168–69
  settings 45–46
connecting to another
  computer 60
Control menu 4, 47
Control Panel 51–52
copying............................ 48–50, 58
counting words 51
creating databases 19, 53, 81–82
Cue Cards 51
currency symbols 51–52
customizing toolbars 52

cutting 53

D

data
  copying 48–49
  entering 64–65
  moving 103
database forms
  about 81–82
  aligning fields 116
  borders.................................. 26
  charts 35–36
  protecting 120, 170
  text 65
databases
  about 10–11
  calculations 128
  creating 19, 53, 81–82
  default entries 65
  form view 84
  formulas 64
  list view 95
  maximum records 125
  merging into word processor
    document..............99–100, 173
  printing................................ 118
  problems.......................... 170–71
  See also database forms
data bits 46
date and time functions 54
dates 54, 73, 80, 146
dBASE 54, 69
default entries 65
default tab stops 154
default templates 156
deleting 55–56
dependents 56
depreciation calculations 74
dialing phone numbers 56, 60
DIAL message 151
dialog boxes 57

documents
    about 57
    closing 44
    creating 2–3, 104, 149
    exporting 69
    naming 134
    opening 2–3, 108, 149, 171
    saving 134
document windows 4–5, 58
dollar sign ($) 16, 51, 102
downloading files 142
draft-quality printing........ 117, 173
drag-and-drop 48, 58
Draw 58–59

E

Easy Connect 60
editing 60–61
Edit menu
    Clear 67
    Clear Field Entry 55
    Clear Formula 67
    Copy 43–44, 50, 144
    Cut 43–44, 53, 103
    Data Labels 39
    Field Name 16, 17
    Fill Down 73
    Fill Right 73
    Fill Series 73
    Find 75, 76, 90
    Go To 25, 86
    Legend/Series Labels 38
    Paste 43, 50, 103, 114
    Paste Special 49, 50, 114
    Paste Text 142, 169
    Redo 125
    Replace 126–27
    Series 40
    Titles 38
    tools 178–79
    Undo 161
embedding objects 62, 63

ending lines 63
endnotes 64
end of document, moving to ... 138
end-of-line mark ...63, 77, 105, 146
entering
    data 64–65
    numbers 65
    text 65
envelopes 19, 66, 109
equal sign (=) 64, 83
erasing 67
ERR() function 68
ERR message 68, 92
error-checking protocol 121
errors
    communications 168–69
    databases 170–71
    files 171–72
    printing 172–74
    spreadsheets 173–76
EXACT() function 158
Excel. *See* Microsoft Excel
exiting Microsoft Works 68
exporting documents 69
extended characters 21
extensions 71

F

FALSE value 96
field lines 70, 82
fields
    about 70
    adding 16–17, 82, 120, 170
    default entries 65
    deleting 55, 120
    height 16–17
    hiding................................... 89
    names 70, 82, 86, 120, 170
    placeholders 99, 173
    positioning 116
    protecting 119, 170
    replacing contents 126

fields *(continued)*
    resizing.............................. 131–32
    selecting 139, 140
    width 16–17
File menu
    Close 44
    Create New File 60, 81, 104, 149
    Exit Works 68
    Open Existing File 108
    Page Setup 64, 70, 87,
        100, 110–12
    Print 66, 82, 97, 98, 117–18
    Printer Setup 117
    Print Preview 118
    Save 71, 134
    Save As 69, 71, 94, 134, 156
    Save Workspace 135
    Templates 23, 94, 149, 156
    tools 178
    WorksWizards 19, 53, 72, 94,
        149, 165
filenames 71
File Organizer WorksWizard 72
files
    copying 72
    deleting 55, 72
    importing 69, 108
    moving..................................... 72
    naming................................ 71, 72
    opening 72
    sending and receiving..... 141–43
filling cells 73
filtering records. *See* queries;
    records, finding
financial functions 74
finding 75–77
fonts 24, 29–31, 77, 93, 161, 173
footers 87–88, 100
footnotes 78–79
Format menu
    Add Border.............................. 32
    Alignment............................ 20, 175
    AutoFormat 23
    Border 25–26

Format menu *(continued)*
    Columns 157
    Column Width 45
    Field Size 131
    Field Width 16, 89, 131
    Font And Style 30
    Horizontal (X) Axis 31, 32
    Number 80, 85, 136, 159, 171
    Paragraph 26–27, 92,
        94-95, 113
    Patterns And Colors 32, 33,
        143–44
    Picture/Object 176
    Protection 119, 120, 170, 175
    Record Height 16, 131
    Row Height 133
    Show Field Name 70
    Snap To Grid 116
    Tabs....................................... 155
    tools 183–85
    Two Vertical (Y) Axes 31
    Vertical (Y) Axis 31, 32
formatting
    about 79–80
    characters 24, 29–31, 93, 161
    charts 31–33
    copying 49
    dates and times 54, 159
    logical values 96
    numbers 51–52, 80–81, 115,
        135–36, 171
    spreadsheets 23
form letters 19
Form Letter WorksWizard 81
forms. *See* database forms
formula bar 8, 60, 83
formulas
    about 83–84
    calculating 27, 100
    copying 49
    entering 64
    erasing...................................... 67
    text string 158
form view 16–17, 84, 162

fractions 85
functions
   about 85–86
   date and time 54
   financial 74
   informational 92
   logical 96
   lookup and reference 96
   mathematical and
     trigonometric 101
   statistical 150
   text 158

G

Gallery menu
   commands 41
   tools 182–83
General Protection Fault 171
go to 86
GPF 171
gridlines 32, 34, 87, 174

H

handshake 46
headers 87–88, 100
help 89
Help Cue Cards command .. 51, 89
hiding fields 89
hiding records 90
hyphenation 90–91, 146

I

IF() function 96
importing files 69
inches 94
indents 92, 133
informational functions 92
inserting columns and rows 93

Insert menu
   Bookmark Name 25
   Chart 35, 62
   ClipArt 18, 42
   Database Field 99
   Delete Page Break 110
   Delete Record 56
   Delete Record/Field 55, 56
   Delete Row/Column 55
   Delete Selection 55
   Drawing 59
   Field 17
   Footnote 78
   Function 86
   Note-It 106
   Object 62, 63, 107
   Page Break 110
   Range Name 104
   Record 18
   Record/Field 17, 18
   Rectangle 26
   Row/Column 93
   Special Character .. 111, 146, 160
   Spreadsheet/Table 62, 153
   tools 181–82
   WordArt 164
insertion point 4, 93
interest calculations 74
INT() function 101
ISNA() function 92
italic characters 30, 93

K

keeping paragraphs together 113
Kermit protocol 121

L

labels. *See* charts, labels; mailing
  labels
landscape orientation 111

LCD display 109
leading zeros 171
left alignment 20
letterheads.................................... 94
line spacing 94–95
lines, ending 63
linking 37, 62
lists, bulleted 26–27
lists, in dialog box 57
list view 16–17, 95, 162
locking cells and fields 119
LOG() function 101
logical functions 96
logical values, formatting 96
logos 163–64
lookup and reference functions . 96
Lotus 1-2-3 .... 69, 96

macros 136–37
mailing labels 19, 97–98
mail merge 99–100, 173
manual calculation 100
manual page breaks 110
margins 100
mathematical functions 101
maximum records..................... 125
menu bar 4
merging 99–100, 173
Microsoft Draw 58–59
Microsoft Excel 69, 101
Microsoft Word 69, 102
Microsoft Works
    documents for other
        versions 69
    exiting 68
    filename extensions 71
    icons x
    sharing data with other
        applications 144
    starting 149
millimeters 94

mixed cell references................. 102
modem setup 102–3, 168
mouse
    drag-and-drop 58
    pointers 109
    selecting text 141
moving 58, 103

NA() function 92
N/A message 92
names 84, 86, 104
naming charts 35
new documents 2–3, 104, 149
newspaper-style columns 157
next page 118, 138
nonbreaking hyphens 91, 146
nonbreaking spaces 77, 105, 146
nonprinting characters 105
Note-It 106
numbering pages 111, 146
numbers
    entering 65
    formatting 51–52, 80–81,
        115, 135–36, 171
    series 73
NUM message 151

object linking and embedding . 107
objects
    about 107
    copying 50
    creating 62–63, 144
    deleting 55
    embedding and linking 62, 63
    moving.................................... 103
    resizing................................... 132
    selecting 140
OFFLINE message 151

OLE 107
opening documents 2–3, 108, 149, 171
operators 83, 158
optional hyphens 91, 105, 146
Options dialog box ... 109, 147, 151
orientation 111
OVR message 151

P

page breaks 77, 110, 172
page numbers 111, 146
pagination 112
panes 5, 163
paragraph breaks 113
paragraph marks ... 21, 77, 105, 113
paragraphs 113
paragraph spacing 94–95
parity 46
pasting 114
patterns 114, 143–44
percentages 115
Phone menu
    Dial 56
    Easy Connect 60
    Hang Up 168
    tools 186
phone numbers 19, 56, 60, 115
phone settings 115
picas 94
pictures 18, 50
    See also ClipArt Gallery; Draw; objects
pie chart labels 39
PI() function 101
placeholders 99, 173
PLAY message 151
points 30, 94, 116
portrait orientation 111
precedents 116
previous page 118, 138
printer, selecting 117

printing
    about 117–18
    forms 82
    charts 32
    mailing labels 97–98
    problems 172–74
print preview 118
PROPER() function 158
protecting
    cells and fields 119, 170, 175
    documents 108
    form designs 120, 170
protocol 121

Q

queen of England 121
queries 90, 121–24
query sentences 123–24
query view 123–24, 162
quitting Microsoft Works 68

R

radio buttons 57
range 104, 124, 139
read only 108
REC message 151
receiving files 141–42
receiving text 28
records
    about 125
    adding 18
    deleting 56
    editing 61
    finding .... 75–76 (see also queries)
    grouping 129
    hiding 90
    selecting 140
    sorting 129, 145
redo 125
relative cell references 125

replacing 126–27
reports 128–30
report view 130, 162
resizing 131–32
right alignment 20
rows
    about 133
    deleting 55
    height 20, 133
    inserting 93
    selecting 140
    sorting 145
ruler 6, 109, 133, 154

S

saving 134–35
scientific notation 135–36
scripts 136–37
scroll bars 5, 138
scrolling 5, 138
searching. *See* finding; replacing
selecting 139–41
sending files 141, 143
serial ports 46
series, chart 35
series of numbers or dates 73
Settings menu
    Communication 45–46, 168
    Modem 102–3, 168
    Phone 115
    Terminal 157, 169
    tools 186
    Transfer 121, 169
shading 143–44
sharing data 144
SIN() function 101
sizing handles 131, 132
Slide to Left option 20
sorting 145
spaces, nonbreaking 105, 146
spacing between lines and
    between paragraphs 94–95

special characters ... 21, 76–77, 146
spelling checker 147–48
split bar 163
splitting windows 163
spreadsheets
    about 6–9, 148
    errors 173–76
    printing 118
spreadsheet view 148
starting Microsoft Works 149
Startup dialog box 2–3, 149
statistical functions 150
status bar 5, 109, 150–51
stop bits 46
strikethrough characters 30
subscript characters 30
SUM() function 24, 150
superscript characters 30
switching windows 152
symbols 21
synonyms 159

T

tables 152–54
tabs 77, 105, 133, 154–55
tab-separated text 69
templates 2, 23, 94, 149, 156
terminal settings 157
text
    capturing 28
    in charts 37–40
    columns 157
    copying 50
    deleting 56
    editing 61
    entering 65
    exporting documents as 69
    finding 76–77
    functions 158
    moving 103
    replacing 127
    selecting 141

text *(continued)*
    sending and receiving 142–43
text string formulas 158
thesaurus 159
time functions 54
times 146, 159–60
toolbar 5, 52, 160, 178–88
tools .... x, 178–88
Tools menu
    Capture Text 28
    Create New Chart 33
    Create New Query 122
    Create New Report 128
    Customize Toolbar 52, 183
    Delete Query 123
    Delete Report 130
    Dial This Number 56
    Edit Script 137
    End Capture 28
    End Recording 136
    Envelope And Labels .. 66, 97–98
    Hyphenation 90–91
    Manual Calculation 100
    Name Chart 35
    Options 109, 147, 151
    Receive File 142
    Record Script 136
    Send File 141
    Send Text 143
    Sort Records 129, 145
    Sort Rows 145
    Spelling 147
    Thesaurus 159
    tools 187
    Word Count 51
Tool Tips 160, 180
transfer protocol 121
trigonometric functions 101
TrueType 161
TRUE value 96
typefaces. *See* fonts
types of charts 40–41

underline characters 30, 161
undo 125, 161
units of measure 94, 109
unlocking cells and fields 119, 170, 175

values 50, 161
View menu
    All Characters 113
    Apply Query 123
    Chart 40, 41, 61, 162
    Display As Printed 32
    Draft 162
    Field Lines 70
    Form 162
    Gridlines 87
    Headers And Footers 87–88
    Hide Record 90
    List 162
    Normal 162, 176
    Page Layout 157, 162, 176
    Query 162
    Report 129, 130, 162
    Ruler 133
    Show All Records 90
    Spreadsheet 40, 148, 162
    Switch Hidden Records 90
    Toolbar 160
    tools 179–80
    Wrap For Window 162, 165
    Zoom 166
views 162, 176

WCM extension 71
WDB extension 71

wildcards 123
Window menu
   Cascade 132
   Split 163
   Tile 132
   tools 188
windows
   application 4–5, 21
   document 4–5, 58
   moving 47
   panes 5, 163
   resizing 47, 132
   saving positions 135
   splitting 163
   switching 152
WKS extension 71
Word for Windows. *See* Microsoft
   Word
word processor
   about 6–7
   merging database
     records 99–100, 173
WordArt 163–64
WordPerfect 69, 164
words, counting 51

word wrap .... 16?
workspace 4, 109, 132, 135,
   149, 165
WorksWizards .... 2, 19, 149, 16?
WPS extension .... 7?
Wrap Text option .... 2(
Write .... 69, 16(

X

Xmodem protocol .... 12?

Y

Ymodem protocol .... 12?

Z

zeros, leading .... 17?
ZIP codes .... 17?
Zmodem protocol .... 12?
zooming .... 118, 16(